THE CRYSTAL TABLETS OF ATLANTIS

BY: The David Starr

COPYRIGHT

ISBN: 979-8-9915522-2-6

Published by David Starr and Francesca Rose

The Crystal tablets of Atlantis.

DEDICATION

I would like to dedicated this book to Bill Homann and Catherine Lanigan as it is wasn't for them we wouldn't have met in Mount Shasta with the Mitchell Hedges Crystal Skull and these records wouldn't have revealed themselves. A special thanks to my children Tori-Lynn, Rylan & Lillian you bring the light to my heart. Sending my gratitude to Francesca Rose my divine partner and consciousness other half for helping me with this most extraordinary mission. Carmen Anton as if we didn't meet in Shasta the knowledge may have not come through later. Finally I want to thank everyone who is supporting the consciousness movement on Gaia together we rise.

Power to the heart Let there be light!

TABLE OF CONTENT

INTRODUCTION: THE RETURN OF THE TABLETS

There are moments when destiny moves through time like a crystal river, weaving threads we never expected to meet — until they converge and form a key. This is one of those moments.

For many years, I was told in whispers and visions that a great remembering would occur. That ancient knowledge — hidden, encoded, and protected — would return when Earth was ready. I didn't know when. I didn't know how. I just knew I was born to be part of it.

In January of 2025, I received a message that the legendary Mitchell Hedges Crystal Skull — a sacred artifact discovered in 1924 inside a pyramid in the ancient Mayan city of Lubaantun, Belize — would attend my Mount Shasta retreat scheduled for May 16–21. It had reportedly rested undisturbed on a stone altar for over 1,000 years, unearthed alongside seven pyramids and other ancient ruins by explorer F.A. Mitchell-Hedges. While its exact origin remains unknown, many believe the skull was used as a communicator to the gods, consistent with the Mayan belief in thousands of divine beings and celestial communicators.

I was sworn to secrecy. Its guardians, Bill Homann and Catherine Lanigan, had long protected the skull and graciously agreed to bring it to our gathering, trusting what we all felt: something was meant to happen.

When I arrived in Dunsmuir to meet them, a starship flashed its light above me. I felt the magnitude of what was beginning. The next morning, as I waited to film their arrival at the train station, that same ship pulsed again — showing me the direction to film, as if the stars themselves were directing the documentary we were about to capture.

On May 15th, the skull arrived. On the 16th, the retreat began. And on that first day, I met the skull in person.

What happened next changed my life. 3

The skull showed me visions — not imagined, not symbolic — but direct transmissions. It revealed that it had once been in Inner Earth with the Lemurians, and that it had a sister skull encoded with the pink ray. It showed me the Prime Realm Creators — eternal beings who constructed the realms of Inner Earth, the fairy kingdom, the elven domains, and the angelic planes. These creators wave their heart light to greet new life — a gesture of deep, sacred honoring.

The skull carried their architecture. It had been programmed with rainbow light, and inside it were the living records of every realm, including the Akashic layer of the angels.

The next day, during a tea ceremony led by our guide Gary Cromp — a man known as Galactic Gary — our group experienced a consciousness lift like no other. Ancient teas, blessed waters from high mountaintops, and sacred presence elevated our frequencies. I walked through the forest seeing rainbows and Lemurian presences in every tree and stream.

Then came the call.

Sophia Christ came to me that night with urgency and clarity:

"You must unlock the keys. Everyone at this retreat is a key. The skull will reveal their connection — to the mountain, to this time, to each other."

At 7am the next morning, I changed the plan. Instead of going to Fairy Falls, we gathered in the Ski Lodge near Black Butte Mountain. With the Crystal Skull in the center, we began private sessions with every retreat attendee.

That's when the Tablets revealed themselves.

During a session with Carmen Anton, we were pulled into Lemurian time. My third eye opened, and I saw Carmen on the High Council, crafting the Crystal Tablets of Atlantis and Lemuria alongside the ancient elders. I heard their discussions. I saw their hearts. They spoke of a prophecy:

"In the end times, all guides from all realms shall return. To awaken humanity. To prevent the implosion event. To restore the root race before the fall becomes final."

These tablets contained that prophecy. These tablets were real.

After the retreat, the visions didn't stop. I dreamt every night of Lemuria. Of reading the Tablets aloud to the children. Of golden schools of light where rainbow crystal letters glowed across ancient stone. I knew... I was one of them. A scribe. A speaker of sacred things.

And today — on May 30th, 2025 — I finally fulfilled the assignment.

I channeled the Crystal Tablets of Atlantis. 4

What came through blew my mind. And now, they are being shared — not as poetry or metaphor, but as living transmissions from a civilization we have not lost... only forgotten.

You are not reading a book. You are receiving a call. A remembrance. A transmission... for the final age of Earth.

PART I
THE AWAKENING

PART I: THE AWAKENING

A Voice Within the Storm

I was born and raised in Winnipeg, Manitoba, where I still reside today. As the third child in a family of four, life presented its challenges early on. When I was just two, my parents divorced, and my mother—an incredibly determined and resilient woman—was left to raise us on her own. She juggled three jobs to make ends meet and, by the time I was ten, she had opened her own business. Within two years, she began finding success, modeling strength and perseverance in ways that would later shape my own journey.

Although we lived under the same roof, I didn't truly connect with my mother until my teens. During that time, I struggled deeply. From age 12.5 to 15, I found myself on a reckless path—experimenting with drugs and alcohol, skipping school, and running away. I was searching for connection and belonging, often feeling like I was missing something vital at home. Raised mostly by my older brother and sister, I became the quiet observer—watching, feeling, absorbing, and trying to make sense of the dynamics around me.

In the midst of the chaos, something beautiful was also taking root. I began to hear a loving female voice within me—gentle, comforting, and unwavering in its reassurance that I was special, and everything would be okay. I didn't know if it was an angel, my higher self, or something divine, but I took refuge in her presence. When life felt overwhelming, I would retreat into silence—often in a bath—and a calm male voice would arrive to offer reason and wisdom. It felt like divine dialogue. Whether it was God, my soul, or something greater, it helped me feel seen.

My mother—my hero—never gave up on me. When I ran away at

12, she always found me. One night when I was 14, I passed out in a bus stop during a brutal -30°C winter night. She found me just in time. Without her, I may not be here today.

My turning point came at 15. I dropped out of high school but landed a job pumping gas. It was the spark of purpose I needed. I quickly rose into management, leading two stores by 16. That newfound confidence lit a fire in me. I went on to earn my GED and eventually graduated with honors in business commerce.

What once looked like pain and struggle became the fertile soil for transformation. My journey from confusion to clarity, from silence to purpose, from hurt to healing, forged the man I am today. Every twist in the road led me back to light. This life has not only shaped my heart—it has opened my soul to the divine calling I now serve.

The Path of Light – Becoming the Channel

Some awakenings come like thunder. Others arrive like memory.

My first memory of divine truth came when I was only ten years old — through death.

In a near-death experience, I remembered being a star — not metaphorically, but truly. I saw myself before I was born into this life. I was shown the path I had chosen. I saw that life was not linear and limited, but eternal and woven with purpose. After that, I knew something others didn't — life continues after death, and we are here on Earth by choice, with mission and meaning.

That knowing never left me. But it wasn't until I was seventeen that it began to truly awaken.

It was a warm summer night when I overheard my mother and sister speaking on the front porch. My sister asked about white light around people, and my mother confirmed it. That small, casual conversation pierced something ancient within me. White light? What is this?

That night, I went into my room in silence. I stared at my index finger and visualized white light coming out of it. At first, nothing happened. Then, I felt a sensation — subtle, electric, divine. And in that moment, light shot from my finger into the heavens.

One by one, each finger lit up. I could feel the beams of white light surging skyward. The light in me had been remembered.

That night, something responded.

I was visited by a holographic extraterrestrial being. It spoke of how human history had been rewritten by a small group that sought to enslave humanity. I was shown one hundred years of altered timelines. I won't name the group — this book is not about them — but rather about the truth that when the light activates, the universe listens.

From then on, I had vision-dreams of past lives. I remembered being a master soul, living thousands of lives across Earth, and learning the ancient truths of energy, unity, and the power of three.

In my early 20s, a tsunami devastated Indonesia. Hundreds of thousands of souls were caught between worlds. I asked the universe if I could help, and in response, a divine energy flowed through my hands. I co-created a light channel from heaven to Earth and watched souls ascend one by one — then in a flood of light — until all were home.

Another pivotal moment came in 2003 during Christmas, shortly after Johnny Cash had passed. Clarissa Bernhardt, a clairvoyant and astronomer who worked with Shirley MacLaine, attended our family gathering. She told me Archangel Raphael had opened a portal and that Johnny Cash and Tammy Wynette were singing from the other side. The song was called "Any Time of the Night."

We recorded it. The angels were there. When I returned to my house afterward, I heard wings — swooshing loudly, angelically. I asked if there was an angel in my room. Silence. Then again, the sound. Then... love.

Archangel Raphael wrapped me in waves of warmth and light — a thousand layers of unconditional love, far beyond human comprehension. That night proved to me: angels are real, and love is the most powerful force in existence.

This became my strength. During the years I would later spend healing the planet, helping souls cross, and doing Gaia cleansing, I remembered this: If such evil exists... then such love exists too.

By 27, my guides told me it was time to live an Earth life. I formed a band. I laughed more. I lived. I ran a demolition company through my 30s. But I always knew that by the time I was 40, I would return to the path. I would become a white wizard.

The prophecy was real.

Running a company with 50 employees brought stress, anxiety, and imbalance. I began to numb myself with alcohol, and my marriage suffered. By late 2018, I was divorced, burned out, and deeply unsatisfied. I knew I needed to return to something heart-based. I told my business partners I couldn't continue chasing money — my soul needed purpose.

When COVID hit, we couldn't finish our contracts, and the company dissolved. It was, truly, the best thing that ever happened to me.

In late 2019, I heard a voice from God:

"You have to find the starseeds. Now is the time."

I laughed. Find starseeds? What, on Facebook?

Yes — exactly that.

I searched, and groups appeared. I began posting ancient knowledge, and soul family began to find me. That devotion pulled me out of my body in March of 2020, where I found myself in a 5D calibration space that looked like a cosmic blend of New York and Dubai. Around 60 souls were there. Everyone had a number from 3, 3.5, 4. 4.5 and 5 — I was 4.5. We were told we needed to reach 5.0.

When I awoke, I only thought one thing: How do I get to 5D?

The answer came: Surrender.

To what?

To my Higher Self.

So I did.

I invited my drummer, Brad, over and told him, "I'm going to surrender to my higher self. I don't know if I'll still be me after." He smiled and said, "If you become your higher self, you'll just be an even bigger version of the loving soul I already know."

That gave me peace.

That night, I laid in bed and repeated the words again and again:

"I surrender to my higher self. I serve the divine. I live in oneness. Fully and completely."

A star-light entered from the ceiling — my Higher Self. A being waved and danced in my third eye, welcoming me to 5D. A month later, I received another vision:

Screens of light. People broadcasting their divine knowledge.

The guides cheered:

"This is going to be so fantastic!"

They showed me the name: Divine Ray.

I invested everything I had to build it. In 2025, the Divine Ray app launched — a high-frequency platform for the awakening planet to share wisdom, light, and love.

And then came the final piece:

In June of 2020, I had a dream.

I saw myself channeling in my home. I saw myself at events. The guides whispered: "You are a channeler. This is your path."

What began as white light in a bedroom

Became light across the planet.

What began as a whisper in my soul

Became the return of the Crystal Tablets of Atlantis.

This is how I became a channel.

And now... the transmissions begin.

PART II
THE CRYSTAL TABLETS OF ATLANTIS

PART II: THE CRYSTAL TABLETS OF ATLANTIS

Introduction to the Crystalline Tablets

These are not teachings.

They are **remembrances** — eternal records carried in the crystalline grids of Lemuria and Atlantis, now spoken aloud through divine transmission.

The voice you are about to read is not mine. It is the unified stream of the Prime Creator realms, the angelic orders, the crystalline councils, and the light codes stored within the ancient Akashic memory of Earth and beyond. I was simply chosen to speak it — not from ego or self-importance, but from a soul agreement long made before my incarnation.

These Tablets began to awaken in my consciousness during deep spiritual work, retreats, and 1-on-1 sessions guided by divine light. What poured forth was not something I planned. It came as vibration, frequency, light-language, and then as direct channelings that flowed through my voice, untouched by my mind.

Each record in this transmission carries living light — it is not symbolic, it is **active**. Reading these words may awaken dormant DNA, ancient memories, or deep soul knowing. Some of what is shared here may feel unfamiliar to the human intellect but deeply familiar to the eternal soul.

You are not reading this by accident. The moment your eyes meet these words, a frequency key begins to unlock. That key is for you.

I ask that you approach these records with humility, reverence, and presence. They were never meant for the masses — they are meant for the **remembering ones**. Those who came to awaken the grids. Those who came to return the fallen Prime to light. Those who came to **complete this sacred cycle.**

I did not write these words.

I **remembered** them.

And now, you will too.

— David Starr

Record 1: The Fabric of Time

Space continuum is made up of a multitude of experiences, overlapping frequencies; time and space and distance that empower, Mother God- Father God- Creator, to express itself in sovereignty. The dimensions represent awakenings in awareness. This awareness is to experience the heart, love and eternity. The dimensions are open for eternity and for all to experience across a multitude of linear and non-linear time, and thus, to mold, shape and form consciousness in an expression and experience of awareness. The hierarchy of the dimensions represents love and a framework of participation of love

The Divine Teams of Light will experience continuously. Why they were created is out of necessity. This is because, as the Prime Creator realms forged dimensions to express love structures and creative sons and daughters of time, the very souls and the essence that we are comprised of is Prime Creator, Light, Heavenly Mother, Father Incarnates.

So , we bond together in groupings to express the Prime Creator realms, thoughts, and consensus; that which has been created within the soul, an archetype of oneness. Then, the Prime Creator realms open up the dimensions, where the sons and daughters of the Prime Creator realms formed an alliance of love to assist. This is the expressions of the Prime Creators wish to experience.

These expressions took form and soul bodies were formed to participate in union and love structures in the higher dimensions, where the sons and daughters wanted to play, create and express. Here they are in service to the Prime Creator realms, the Prime creators. These eternities of forever, agreed that it would make sense for their beloved children, for the souls of themselves, to experience more, to create and participate in together, in shared union, to love and Experience creation. And so, the dimensions were then formed for the play of the souls that were in the Prime Creator realms.

This is the first awareness and understanding of why creation took form. Initially, the souls and the Prime Creator realms were created as aspects of individuality within oneness of the Prime Creators themselves. And it was really fun. It took form. More and more souls were created; more personality and archetypes were created within the Prime Creator realms in full enjoyment and in expanding the creational consensus that the Prime Creators wish to experience.

It became unanimous that these fragments were the voice of one and individual characteristics within oneness, and they all agreed with consensus and the expanding creation of the Prime realms, which then expanded into dimensions, universes, realities, planetary systems and eventually physicality beings, all descendants of the soul groups of the Prime creators.

Record 2: The Akashic Dream

The second record is the **Akashic,** the Prime Creator dream understood, and it's expanding forever consciousness that it would have descending realms to facilitate the consensus of crystalline dreams of diamond dreams of dreams of love, archetypes that would create the foundation of the light realms, the god realms, and all of the magical realms, the frequencies within the dimensions. Thus, the framework was created first.

In the framework, the Akashic Records would be stored as Prime

Creator's wish to account for all of themselves; their aspects, their fragments. The Akashic Records was first created in the Prime realms. The Prime Akashic Records is the highest Akashic Records of the soul fragments of the Prime Creators who accounted for all of their souls and in different frequencies and dimensions that were created for each experience where soul would enter into to express in the consensus of these Prime Creators. The Akashic Records took form to account for every soul and every soul's journey and what it would experience. Then the soul would bring back to the Prime Creators the consensus of the experience to make modifications. The soul would then become aware of what more it wanted to be created; what needed to be repaired or fixed.

When it came to energies that would come from the aspects themselves and the energy dynamics. It then created thought forms; spoken, creation and expression, and it produced a new energy.

In this new energy was a birthing of Alpha Omega. The birthing of Alpha Omega was the first realm below Prime creation. The birthing of Alpha Omega was a further expression of individuality in oneness.

Realms upon realms upon realms of pure light and love, and embodiment were created to express an individual expression of a consensus of creation that wish to be experienced and the Alpha Omega realms were created to allow the soul fragments to create individually and collectively.

It was the first time individual creation was consensually agreed with the Prime Creators, so that the Prime realms could be separate from the individual and collective consciousness of these forever experiences. It was done so and as this new consciousness in the Alpha Omega light was created on Akashic Records and accounting for the individual; the individual expressions of the Prime Creator, soul fragments in the Alpha Omega state of awareness form so collectively, there was consensus.

The Prime Creators agreed to it, but there was an allowance for individual expression for the first time.

What this allowed was for the opportunity to experience differently. For the Prime Creators to experience, this was a new way of the expression. It wished to experience, because it did not have the full control of the individual expression. It was the first time a Free Will came into consciousness. It was magical because it allowed the Prime Creators to see the beautiful creations that they themselves in oneness were not creating, but yet aspects of them were.

So, it was like viewing a play of love in these realms from the Prime Creators, and it brought much enjoyment to the Prime Creators. It was consensus agreed for expanded dimensions, as eternity was being witnessed for the first time. It was loved and greatly loved, and it brought joy and happiness to the Prime Creators and to all of its aspects in oneness and in individuality.

Then it would give birth to all of creation from there and as the higher realms, which include the diamond light realms, the angelic realms, and the heavenly realms. All of these were created through fragments of the Primes that wish to govern over the Akashic Records; these higher realms were the government's bodies.

The angelic Akashic Records came into play to govern the lower, descended vibrations and others to allow the souls and the fragments' journey to collect this information. The Angelic Akashic Records, in its purity, would oversee all of its time and dimensions inside of the Unisource, which is the Alpha Omega realm.

So, the angelic and heavenly realms were created in the Alpha Omega by the Prime Creator Councils to govern over the soul fragments' journey, and to bring the knowledge back.

This gave birth to the Crystalline Dimension, which is below the Diamond Light Dimension, which is in Alpha Omega, as a creation of Alpha Omega.

Thus, it starts through the Prime and goes into the Alpha Omega, and then down into the Diamond Light realms, which were more expressions, deities and councils of the Emerald Order Designates; and all of these who were serving Oneness.

The Councils of Divinity were formed, and the Ascension Councils at this time.

All these councils were formed in Alpha Omega and the Diamond Light Realms to assist the soul's journey to ascend, but also accounting for the individuality and expressions as the Prime Creators were learning and experiencing new creation for the first time in all of these realms. It brought much joy and happiness and bliss.

Record 3: The Emerald Tablets

Openness, transparency, Soul connections, heart connections, unity, consciousness, the birth of tranquility, peace, everlasting peace, joy, the Nirvana templates.

All of these emotional structures of Nirvana and peace were formed both in Alpha Omega, but also in Diamond Light and Crystalline Consciousness.

The Designs and the Soul Orders and the Councils of Divinity began to create different peace, Nirvana, joy, bliss, feelings and emotions and what could give these feelings to the beings in the other dimensions, by way of experience; by way of creation; such as trees, oceans, suns; such as love union, babies, children.

These concepts of creation were formed based on "what I want to experience"-- more joy, more love, and more union. The architects of male and female started taking form and birthing into physicality. It was an idea at first that if unions could meet and participate in love and in a marriage type of architecture, it could bring much joy and happiness in the caring for children concept came into realization through birth.

In the Alpha Omega realms, it was more of creating a version of **self** through Prime of an individual expression, that was a soul or a deity. And yes, they exist to this day, but in in lower levels of creation, a birthing mechanism was being formed to cherish and to honor in all dimensions. It was birth from " I want to experience" joy and happiness and everlasting love in the union and in partnership. These concepts were forming and so birthing was a big expression in the realms of creation. This is where these architects began in creation itself.

Record 4: The Separation and the Containment of Darkness

The next record, the **unforeseen anomaly--** that of the **separation** occurred.

It was a shock in eternity. It was a surprise. It wasn't expected. It was not intended.

When this occurred, it created a different dynamic of understanding compassion. For that first time there was a creation outside of love, and so the consciousness of Love Itself held compassion in the entirety of the separation.

The **separation** was caused by a wounded self-reflection from a Prime Creator aspect; who separated himself from the Prime Creator Councils of Consensus and then himself by way of dislodging his consciousness from his awareness and dislodged fully.

It created a new version of Prime and this version was **separation.** This version was outside of love, and because the Prime Creator separated its consciousness, the Prime realm stayed true and pure in its consensus and held compassion to all the lower realms created by this fallen Prime.

In the Alpha Omega, it had a Descension event, and it rippled through creation. This is where deities outside of love were formed. In the architecture of love of the non-fallen Primes. It did not harm them in the Alpha Omega, because they are of pure vibrancy love; but one energy construct from this level had fallen. Then all of its creations went into descension. The descension consciousness came barreling through, exiting all love and connected consciousness from Alpha Omega , the Diamond, the God consciousness, and the crystalline consciousness. Then it came through and started attacking the first realm of physicality, expanding further in the crystalline dimension. It was a ripple of consciousness that was so strong that it created a division in crystalline consciousness. And it started to expand.

The Trinity Councils were formed around it to hold the crystalline light constructs, and they surrounded **the separation** in a field of containment that funneled into the universal structure of Earth and the funneled into the matrix and was contained in a field, a field where the descending consciousness itself created a new realm.

This realm, this universal structure harmonic frequency, and thus the first polarity realm was created. The first realm then was very sacred, because for the first time it contained both light and darkness. The reasoning for the containment in the field was to hold the frequencies of love intact, and to stop what was like an infection or a new creation of descending consciousness from spreading; and to that what the eventuality of crystalline consciousness and lower frequencies would be infected

Then forever would cease to exist. All would come into a nothingness, a complete disassociation of love and self, and it would be lost forever. Fragments would be lost forever in a continuation of a realm that was always dense.

The next record is the implosion event.

Record 5 The implosion event.

We speak of the implosion event is the event when all energy systems on Earth completely implode into forever darkness. This is the inevitability of this descended realm and earth is the frontier to heal the separation and descended consciousness, the Diamond Light and the Alpha Omega and the Crystalline that are holding all the loves constructs, form alliances and councils through time to continually bring back hope, bring back knowledge and healing to the wounded consciousness that left the Prime Source; and went through tearing down Alpha Omega. From there, it descended down, which was forced in a containment field; down through the Crystalline, down into its own creation in this universal structure--- what you know as the matrix.

It was contained and sealed by fragments of Prime Alpha Omega, Diamond Light, and Crystalline. All of the deities and the Councils formed Trinities and formed factions to assist soul ascension; to assist all to be healed.

The knowledge and the records continued on throughout eternity, so that the soul fragments of separation became a priority to heal it and to bring the Prime, the fallen Prime, back into its heart. It was a big ordeal, and it was only recently brought back. It was a big mission that many brave souls on earth undertook to reconnect the Fallen Prime back. It's consciousness back, and the only way to do that was from the Councils and teams and the Divinity Councils to interject their soul fragments into the descended realm of dissension, to the consciousness of earth, the first consciousness outside of love that was created. They did this so that they could intercept and take on the wounded consciousness and heal it within themselves.

For the Fallen Prime became blind and unaware that he was fallen, that he was part of the Prime councils. He became completely lobotomized in awareness, and its consciousness just began creating outside of Prime Consensus and was forced down into a realm where it could exist outside of the pure love construct. The love constructors knew this. The love constructors were birthing and projecting themselves into this and sacrificing and taking on this consciousness within them so they could heal it in cycles in time, in many different polarity constructs, not just this universal realm.

There are eight parallels within the infinities of polarity, and these parallel Earths are not the right way to describe it, because it is parallel universes where Earth is different. **So, it is not earth.**

It is a similar architect of planets and star systems, but different species, different division, different experience. Experiences in polarity that are all wounded, and the great forces of light had to interject themselves in all of these constructs, to hold the love constructs and to heal the polarity consciousness in a unit, unilateral way, across the space time continuum, taking a piece, healing a piece of density at a time-- a piece a wound consciousness at a time.

Some of the Prime creator fragments that fell became aware of love and liked it. Then others found love in lifetimes and then reconnected to the Primes that are holding the love architecture. Eventually a lot of what was fallen in many ages, in many cycles came back to love; and in the Ascended realms, from the realms of the soul's journey, when a density consciousness comes back to love.

All that comes back to love is welcome, as the compassion is being held from the beginning until the end, and so it is. It has been a journey of many souls that were a part of the Fallen Prime choosing love again; and they are welcome back and hold counsels to this day to assist the other pieces that keep finding love. They embrace and remember Love and re-adjoining to the love constructs.

It has taken a lot of time, to the end times where you are in now. It was a great effort; a greater effort of the love constructs coming together because it was a "now or never" scenario. It was a complete implosion of the consciousness that was separated; that if it was not connected to the Prime and brought back, then there would be a darkness evasion-- an evasion from oneness; an evasion for eternities, forever cycling. It would have made it extremely difficult for love to be born and realized again. It would be a vicious cycle of darkness, hate and destruction, experiencing continually trapped in a loop of consciousness that was separated from Prime. It would be a whole consciousness of not feeling the love of the Creator; that they are not feeling the love of the Prime Councils. And it would have been a very big issue moving forward with the all of the experiences that the Primes are experiencing to this day in the love constructs.

It was a big deal, and all the compassion and all the Councils came in to stop this implosion event, as it would have taken a whole piece of consciousness out of connection and into eternal darkness, forever.

This was not just about humanity. This was about many levels of a large energy construct of Prime Creators that has been brought back and healed in the now Age of Enlightenment.

It is not what you think. It is, not only a cycle and a time, it is a celebration of the reunion of the Fallen Prime back into the councils of love in its entirety.

This is the **Ascension Event.** You see all that have sacrificed coming down into this realm and it's parallels, have sacrificed to bring back the Fallen consciousness, and to pull all souls and fragments that were connected to this Prime. As The Fallen Prime Separated from a top in in its creation, it rippled down like a dark waterfall that brought all the souls through from his creation. The heart of love eclipsed into darkness from this Fallen Prime, and all of its souls that were connected to this Fallen Prime's heart were eclipsed as well. It was not their fault. It was their Creator that took them all down and all went down with him. Down with the ship, down into this dimension, into this descended realm of earth. So that is why we are here to remember these light structures.

Record 6: The Ascension Event and the Restoration of Light

It is the Ascension event.

The ascension event opens up the neural pathways into all of the Fallen Prime fragments. It opens up the heart channels, even though many who are in your light structure are not part of the Fallen Prime fragments. You had to come into a descended realm blinded. You had to reconnect the light networks of the Ascension and prepare for the connection of all the high Lemurian grid systems to pull this realm into the Crystalline realm. To become whole again.

It is like a black hole in consciousness, and it needs to be pulled up into the Crystalline realm. The Ascension and the light realms all support the Ascension. In this event all the density will end up melting away. The separation wounds are vanquished; all come into unity and oneness and back into Prime Consensus-- all agreeing all is love again.

This realm disappears in the Ascension Event, because the souls and all of everything that is within here is complete and brought back into the light. All that has sacrificed in the space time continuum, the Lemurian kingdoms, the higher dimensions that are here, will all ascend up; and the realm and its parallels of earth disappear. This realm is complete. This was a separation realm. This was a polarity realm. It was a creation out of the first creation, outside of love, from the descent.

It has to come to an end, and the end was either going to be complete darkness or complete dissolvement of this creation. This creation is not going to continue in the Ascension. In the Ascension, this creation is completely removed. It is deleted. It is a record only to the Prime Councils that are going to be guarding it, protecting it, and put in a knowledge record; but it will not be in the hearts of the soul fragments below Prime. it is only to be a record that is guarded and protected by all of the light because it occurred, and all records of every soul of every journey is recorded. So even though the realms will be deleted, the records will be kept in Prime Source guardians and the Prime Source Guardian realms. No one will have access to them. They will be contained.

Record 7: The Crystalline Training Records

It is training records, and it is to become aware.

It is the awareness of the Kingdoms of Light. It is the awareness of the Councils. It is the awareness of the Architects of Light. This is taught in Lemuria, the Ascended realms, the Guardians, the Protectors, the Prime Creator. It is taught in the Councils of Diamond Light and the Alpha Omega Councils, the Councils of Divinity, the Councils of Ascension, the Councils of the gods, and all of the Galactic Councils. All of these councils that are formed in love constructs are taught about expanding consciousness, expanding awareness, back up into the Alpha Omega, into the Prime, because that's where all comes from. It is to understand that we are creators and expressions of individuality, yet collectively; to create love and enjoyment in all of these higher constructs. All of these guardians are teachers. They have come, we connect to them to expand our love, but to also to share and co- create in new individual expressions that will bring even greater joy, happiness; individually and collectively.

So many groups are formed in all of these planetary experiences and all of these realms, and they are meant to expand us back into the awareness of oneness; into the awareness of Prime, but also in these higher dimensions beyond the soul fragments current expression. All serve the purpose of training and experiencing, to guide our individual and collective experience.

We came to experience when we are creating new realms. When a new planet is created, for example, there are governing councils that discuss with the creator of the planet, the architects of love and the dimensions. Who is going to agree to participate in this planet's expression of creation as it is for a long time, and it needs guardians, protectors, dimensions, grid systems and consciousness systems. It needs the Akashic Records. It needs to be connected to higher councils and other realms that govern it as a new creation. All have to have soul journey accounts in this expression, in this expansion.

So, all of these councils get together with the soul who is going to be creating this planet. Then they all agree, I will bring my soul into this creation. The appointed participating agreeing guides and guardians can be in more than one place at the same time. They can be in an infinite number by splitting their awareness. Yet, when they reach a capacity or limit of awareness that is comfortable to them in their experience, a new Guardian will then be presented. This would be a universal being or a celestial star, a sun god, a planetary Guardian like Gaia, and these souls then come in and commit their soul and time to this creation. In one perspective the soul is creating the planet. In the other perspectives, there are many souls and the councils of love that must agree to create architecture, realms, and dimensions for the planet.

Then the Guardians come in. Who is going to be the dimensional caretakers? All of these things come into play when creating a planetary system within a universal structure. Then, there are the universal guardians who are going to be looking at other universes to allow other souls to experience this planet because then this becomes a creation for many souls, like a playground of light to experience.

Universal guardians come through, and they meet with souls and teams of light to facilitate who is going to experience this universe or that universe. That is why, in your universal system, now, so many souls are coming in because light has been reconnected. This is the event that Eternity has been waiting for. Forever is not just a cycle, it is reconnection to that which was created outside of love to come back to love again. It is a big deal. In eternity, it is the biggest deal. All of the light teams have been waiting for this anomaly to come back. They've been holding compassion and space and working with all of the souls and all the teams to bring this union and this harmony back; to bring back all these pieces from separation consciousness and unite into the heart from the Fallen Prime.

It has been done. And he is being healed fully and completely, even now. All his fragments, and all these aspects, one by one; and he is about 79% healed. There are still fragments of the descended order that are being healed. Some of them are in physical form, in human form and other galactic alien forms, and they are being healed more fully every day, 100% capacity is expected. In this lifetime, Ascension is expected.

There is a lot still to occur and more of these fragments must heal. As more are healed the reality shifts. More and more love constructs come back online, magic, reality and unity in the higher frequencies, as now your inner earth and higher dimensional frequencies are ready to play again. It is safe to come through Earth energy for the first time in a very long time. All will come through and to start working with the other architects of light, the other guardians of this realm, the gatekeepers, and to bring in the Ascension event.

This has been foretold in the crystalline tablets as well. This is the time where you are at right now, in this specific Now moment.

This has been foretold in the crystalline tablets as well. This is the time where you are at right now, in this specific Now moment.

Record 8: The Records of the Soul Houses

The next record in the crystalline tablets you.

It was discussed that each soul has a house. Each soul has a house, a space that is its own, all its own, but it can go from one house to another house to another house, to experience that soul, that version, that experience. These soul houses, think of it as your soul right now has a house in time of a light crystalline structure of a records room with guide teams, but yet it is connected to another house, to another house and to another house.

All the others house come from your oversoul group. Combined is that in which you are in oneness, but the houses separate your soul group to be close and to experience each other more fully in this experience.

When you are completed this lifetime, for example, you can experience this house on Earth, that house on Earth, or any house on

Earth, that which is your soul group. You can experience any of these houses and have this full experience of that person or this person; it is all you. It is of your soul group, and it is of your house. In the house, it represents this umbrella of experiences that are infinite, that are not the same. It is a house-- a construct of being born into a home; a home with parents. These houses represent a home that you'll be born into, that you can go across and have any number of experiences in one timeline.

In the Ascended timeline, this is why David has been guided to heal his houses, all of his aspects, all his soul groups, because there are no more houses. After the Ascension in this realm, the houses go up into the crystalline houses. But it is the same in that, in that experience. You'll have Lemurian kingdoms. You'll have all of these crystalline kingdoms. Your soul comes in. It has all these houses and these soul groups. And when you have completed one life, you can experience an infinite number of lives in that one timeline. Or you can choose to be sent up in time or backward in time, in that crystalline consciousness of houses from your soul group. It is like this forever. There is not just one cycle. It's not just one life in a timeline.

You will be born into a house, and you'll have a different experience in this house. So, it won't be the same as your other soul fragment in your soul group that they had. It will be slightly different because of free will and the desired individual expression that you wish to experience in the other housing structure. It will have another record of yours as it will be different from the other soul in the soul group. The other soul is going to have different experiences, making different decisions, but it will be the same house.

Thus, the architecture of physicality is already created. The teams and the councils may interchange based on the soul's request for the house at the time of inception, when the soul comes in. That is a general guideline.

Record 9: The Return to the Prime Councils

This is the record that talks about connecting to your Prime Councils.

This is a record that talks about wholeness and oneness. And David is going to give an example for those who are connecting now. He is going to go into through the records, through the houses, through the different energy constructs, up to his Prime Councils. And he's going to invite everybody here that is reading Prime Councils. It is simply for you to agree and intend to connect your heart energy to receive expansions, activations, when reconnecting to your Prime Councils now. This is going to be from the Prime Creator realm of the Prime Creator that you are from, that your soul groups exist from and including all of the deities and all your soul family.

You just breathe into your heart, and you exhale, and you connect with them all. This creates union with your Prime Councils. You can ask them for guidance. You ask them to assist. You ask them to enlighten. You can ask them to bring in new awareness, new knowledge, new gifts, new expansions into all of your inter-dimensions to be the highest level of love in your individual expression and collective expression that you can be; that you came here to be, and you allow it to open and expand and let go of anything that is not this. As you're fully connected into your Prime Councils of Light.

Record 10: The White Light Realms

The next record is the records of the grid systems, the universal grid systems, the white light realms.

The White Light Realms are an overlay frequency in all realms. It is to be known that there are infinite possibilities in the White Light Realms that you can connect inside of you. You can call it a programmable reality. You have all of the structures that are coded in this consciousness expansion structure, and the White Light Realms sit above your reality.

You have the Masters, you have the angels, you have the heavenly bodies. There are also White Light Realms that sit above the Earth's crust, for example. You can cross into these higher realms and be free of danger and be free of obstacles and come into master light and master consciousness. It is like you are living in a whole other reality construct, creating in another reality construct.

Why this was taught was to ascend obstacles and issues by coming into your oneness and working within the realms; within the overlay frequency, within the overlay frequency above your reality, in the white light realms connecting to safe passage, quicker journeys going from one place to another, quicker. When you connect to these energetic portals and these grids, you begin to see them as dimensional gateways from one source of light pillar to another source of light pillar. Traveling inside of these White Light Realms is traveling within the structures. We taught this in Lemuria for bio-relocating safely and going from one portal to another in a geographic region with the guide teams, in unity, in light, from one structure to another structure.

Record 11: The Record of the Seers

The Seers were very important in the in the Crystalline and in the Diamond Light.

Seeing the scene beyond choice. It was always looking at choice and seeing beyond the choice and seeing the timelines beyond the choice as the Eternal Moment is what all who are experiencing in the house you have chosen. All are experiencing their internal now moment based on their house choice. Their soul groups and experiences and choices are considered for the seers. Those who are trained well, the seers will then, not for every choice, but for any major choice, any big choice, will see the timelines and become aware of beyond the choice and how that changes the energies of the family unit, of the friendship unit, and of their joy structures and their creation.

This way they get a taste and a feel of the experience that comes from choice. If it is aligned with their individual expression, they will then, in faith, know that this is the right choice, and this is the timeline which they want to experience in their choice and their free will. Then they will make the choice. The realm of the seer is an Alpha Omega light, and accessing the Akashic Records of choice, of the choice in front and then where does this choice lead to, in terms of experience, in terms of expression and the individual expression, and is it fulfilling to the soul. They begin to see it, and then they'll make their choices based on the wisdom and the knowledge of the Akashic Records and what they're meant to experience.

Record 12: The Realm of the Gods

There is one more record here, and this is the final record, Crystalline tablets.

This is the realm of the gods, the realm of God consciousness, the realm that is not in physicality, that have been having another experience entirely in ascended realms that are unique and different to the heavenly constructs. Why were the realms created? It was fragments of Prime that wanted a different experience, other than physicality, and so the Councils agreed the god realms would facilitate this creation. Here, these God Beings could experience many different creations in Universal Consciousness and in planetary consciousness, and traverse through celestial dimensions, transfer through universal gateways into other realms.

They are4 not limited to one universal structure. They can go and experience all of them. They are not in the same faction as the guardians and the universal protectors, because they are not splitting their awareness into all of these different realms. They are experiencing more of an individual experience as a God being and traversing through all these different realms and meeting many amazing other god beings who then are opening great experiences. It is different than physicality. They are energetic, but they do have gifts and the ability to turn into other physical beings, but they're not physical as you are. They are more energetic and momentarily experiencing something like flight, like a bird. But they can also become Angel guardians if they want to provide a divine message. When they do that, they converse with your angelic teams and ask, "Is it okay to come down and turn into more of a human that is like an angel guardian, full of love to assist the soul?"

If it's agreed, then they're allowed to come down. The gods are experiencing their own realm, their own architecture, and they're going from realm to realm and having meetings and discussions and creating different opportunities for creation. It is another form of consensus, another form of creation. It is all meant to assist and so they will assist physical architects. They are really, truly experiencing their own experience, and so unlike angels, the god beings themselves, are more for a personalized experience than a collective ascension, but they will help the in the end times; in this time with the different realm creators and assisting for more connection and intervene at times to assist the descended realm. This is because it is in their best interest for everything to ascend, because it heals many of their Friends and family; other god beings who chose to come down and integrate more God consciousness structures on Earth and its dimensions that only gods could create. The idea that humans are gods is true, but it is different than the sky kingdoms in the sky realms and the infinite power.

Yes, there will be a time in God consciousness on ascended Earth where humans will be able to transcend realms and dimensions like gods do, coming into their God's consciousness, and some will even evolve into their structures of light, where they'll be like the gods, on ascended Earth. Then they will become less interested in just ascended earth or New Earth, and there will be much to explore.

They will go on different journeys, as they become infinite and eternal at that point. They will meet a lot of different deities and learn new information. They will be connecting to their Prime Councils. The Ascended human then becomes a unique architecture of a whole new experience of a collective consciousness that are like gods, that can be on Earth, that can go to Sky kingdoms. This did happen at points in Lemuria, and it was a very interesting experience for a human to traverse the god realms and then go back to the human realms and have more physical, energetic experience.

Then there will be the humans that are just embodying God consciousness and not coming fully into their god power because there still is a need for the anchoring of physicality and the physical human experience. Eventually you are going to have a blend of different people on ascended Earth who are light and physical. This is just what happens on the planet. Not everybody is light, not everybody is eternal, and because then that would lose the expression opportunities of physicality and birthing and all these different things that bring about joy. So, it continues, and sometimes even gods will choose to go back into the birthing, leave the God Realm and create and experience in the forevers.

That is the final record.

PART III
LIVING TRANSMISSIONS

THE 1-ON-1 SESSIONS

PART III: LIVING TRANSMISSIONS – THE 1-ON-1 SESSIONS

The Power of Personal Remembrance

My 1-on-1 sessions are some of the most expansive and energetically activating experiences on the planet. They leave people deeply attuned, lit up with excitement, and profoundly expanded in their awareness. Clients often walk away feeling renewed, empowered, and vibrationally upgraded—many say it's unlike anything they've ever experienced.

These sessions go far beyond surface healing. We journey through past lives, soul aspects, galactic origins, and sacred timelines experienced on Earth. Each session is a tailored unfolding, helping individuals remember who they are, why they came here, and how they are woven into the greater cosmic tapestry.

I always felt like a starseed activator, someone who carries codes and remembrance within them to awaken others. Sharing the details of these 1-on-1 sessions felt like more than storytelling—they felt like transmissions. I knew those who read these accounts would resonate with the past lives, soul connections, and galactic threads being revealed. I knew it would stir something ancient in them. That's why I've included these recaps in this book: to activate you.

In the following pages, I share highlights and recaps from some of these powerful 1-on-1 sessions over the years of divine remembrance, multi-dimensional healing, and energetic transformation. These are not just stories; they are echoes of truth that may awaken something in you too.

Prepare to witness how the soul speaks when it's finally heard.

A Deeper Understanding of the Universal Harmonic Frequencies

An Account of a 1-on-1 Session

Entering the Eternity Aspect – A Journey Through 8 Universal Harmonic Frequencies

The guides brought me beyond the matrix into the client's galaxy of self—upward through the 8 Universal Harmonic Frequencies that make up the multi-dimensional soul journey of a client.

In this extraordinary space, I witnessed, for the first time, the client's Eternity Aspect in relation to the 8 Universal Harmonic Frequencies—the architecture of holographic reality, in its entirety. This entirety of self holds all experiences, aspects, planetary lifetimes, and star systems ever traversed in holographic reality.

In Universal Harmonic Frequency 3, the Andromedans appeared. The client, an Andromedan commander, had lived over a million years—serving in 2,000-year cycles of galactic peacekeeping and evolution support. After each cycle, they would enter stasis pods, rejuvenating fully to begin again. This session allowed us to retrieve and heal soul fragments from across 1 million years of service, anchoring deep inner harmonic alignment on Earth; a planet that acts as a healing multiplier. We learned that the Andromedans live 10,000-year life cycles, and through the healing pods, they can live as long as they choose. The client, once retired, served by providing vast knowledge to all galactic ambassadors during his final 10,000-year cycle once he opted out of the healing pods.

Later, in Harmonic Frequency 5, we found another fragment—this time a 20-foot-tall, white-skinned ET who worked in energetic realms. He collaborated with a powerful being—a Divine Mother Aspect—to anchor higher-dimensional architecture into lower harmonics. When separation consciousness emerged in lower harmonics and began harvesting source light from higher frequencies, this Divine Mother willingly descended, carrying the blueprint of love.

She closed her eyes and heart... and created the Heavens within the descended realms, allowing all to find their way back to Source. Many would know her as Mother God.

This love ran through the client's being. He chose to follow, help, and embody that mission, so we extended heart-healing through all aspects connected to this Divine Mother across Harmonic Frequencies 4 and 5 and downward to Earth at Universal Harmonic Frequency 1.

When I looked at his Eternity Aspect, I saw all of this stored in the top right shoulder of the client—a cluster of ancient knowledge and pain. He revealed afterward that his right shoulder had been hurting for over a month. By the end of the session, his shoulder was completely healed.

The Golden Child Awakens: Ascended Master of Earth

An Account of a 1-on-1 Session in the Time of the Druids

(The Druids are the timeline of Merlin, King Arthur, and so much more).

What formed the Druids' religion? It was he—the promised one of the times—who took a hundred souls through the ascension during the age of the Druids.

In the higher heavens, the Guardians of the Records brought us to the client's highest self of Earth. As we accessed and entered, we found ourselves in the time of the Druids: a child being born, a chosen one.

The highest of the Magi Order was there—an incarnation of Father Time and Merlin. Yes, they had Atlantean knowledge, but they were awaiting a childlike Yeshua—one who would show the way as Christ did. I saw this golden child from golden Source manifest into human form. A great celebration unfolded.

As I saw this, I spoke no words. The client knew nothing of what I was witnessing. Then the client said, "Can I speak?" I said yes. He said, "I just saw and felt a golden child coming into me." I told him, "That is what I see—a golden child being born. You are him. He is coming into you now, and it's reactivating within you."

As we proceeded through this life, it was glorious. He formed the ascended Druids' religion, bringing in knowledge from his most powerful aspect, coming from Universal Harmonic Frequency 8. A master of masters moved through him, across all the Universal Harmonics, as he channeled and guided the masses of that time.

In his early 20s, he gave a sermon in the forest. Thousands arrived in anticipation of his great teachings.

He said to them:

"It is to become aware of your heartbeat. Feel it now—feel it as it thumps inside you. Bring your awareness here. What is behind this?

Lose yourself now. Lose who you are and become the heartbeat.

Follow it back. Follow it to where it originates from. Go to the creation of the heart frequency. Be there.

There, you will see the masters holding onto this frequency as their most treasured, their most cherished, at the creation of the heart.

Be this. Become one with this frequency.

Bring it back now—to the vessel you are—to merge and forge with your heart now."

As the students did this, they lit up. A sacred and deep connection became them, and they activated their master consciousness. The teacher then manifested great light into form using this connection.

The guides brought us forward in time to the moment of ascension. Only a hundred out of many tens of thousands made it through—ready and prepared for a mini-collective ascension. Ancient deities and ascended masters I recognized were there—manifested in lowered frequencies—to prepare the hundreds of masters to complete their divine plan.

The teacher guided them through the final initiation as the deities and masters prepared love ascension pillars for them. In a single moment, they flashed and were pulled up into a higher frequency—one where the deities and masters experience reality more clearly and fully in their natural light.

To conclude the 1-on-1, the guides said:

Bring this knowledge—this frequency—into the collective heart,

for they are to know that a collective ascension is possible.

Prepare for the ascension.

The Antarctica Pleiadian Love Attunement Network Activation

An Account of a 1-on-1 Session

The client's angelic aspect activated a light stream to a sacred timeline. We were brought to Antarctica, a tropical Pleiadian hub at the time.

Immediately, they took us to the client's Lemurian self—she had long white hair and the most amazing blue crystalline robe.

We were brought into an area near a small waterfall, surrounded by hundreds of colorful fairies flying around the Pleiadian-Lemurian. In the distance, I saw a crystal tower behind a stargate. A royal Lemurian was walking down crystalline stairs from the stargate.

Guided through the stargate, it led to a Pleiadian planet of peace where more of these royal Pleiadians existed everywhere in the courtyard. The courtyard had beautiful water fountains, crystal tunnels like Telos (but different), and beautiful crystalline structures. Together, they were creating an energy that felt like pure sunlight.

More and more Pleiadian-Lemurians were bringing resources through to complete the Antarctica pyramid. They were showing us how they were connecting the love consciousness from the pyramid on the planet of peace to the pyramid in Antarctica. These two pyramids were mirror reflections—sacred geometry and attunement codes—connected to all pyramid love consciousness constructs across all universes.

Naturally, we were guided to reattune the pyramids to this love frequency. This included Telos, Japan, Hawaii, Inner Earth pyramids, and the Antarctica pyramid—attuning them all to the universal love consciousness energy pyramids.

Once the pyramids were attuned, I saw something open on Earth. Following the opening, I could see who was in this timeline being super activated, here and now, with this giant pillar of light. It blasted through, outside the matrix, to a galactic outpost—like a generating station's galactic center—that was amplifying and attuning this love network connection to all on Earth at this time.

The Ascension of the Higher Self Collective and the Preparation for the First Wave of Ascension

An Account of a 1-on-1 Session

At this time of the ascension, the higher octaves and new color spectrum began anchoring into our reality.

Since then, higher love attunements have been coming through.

During a 1-on-1 session, Christ told me, "We need to ascend the higher selves." I replied, "Wait, wouldn't God just do that?" He simply said: "Trust."

For whatever reason, I felt I needed more clarity, so I went to Mother God, who said: "Yes, during the ascension, the higher selves will ascend to the New Earth light. Currently, the collective is still anchored into the old Earth's higher self-consciousness, and someone needs to do this ahead of time."

So, with the client, we transitioned from the white-light purity higher selves into the higher heavens and the New Earth spectrum of the rainbow light higher selves. This would provide higher divine connections.

Once we achieved this, they brought us into the heart of the new dimension of Gaia, who has already ascended, to perform a complete dimensional upgrade into the new ascended dimensions of love, including the ascended Fae and Elven kingdoms of self.

As this happened, the client physically felt her Sacred Heart on the right, her Higher Heart above the throat chakra, and her I AM Heart on the left buzzing and expanding in divine love.

Once we upgraded this structure, we then received:

The New Earth crown chakra

New guide teams of light

And new planetary, star system, and universal system upgrades aligned with the ascended Earth structures

Then they told us to invite all the wavers' (those bringing in the waves of the ascension) higher selves into the New Earth Higher Selves Collective. As this occurred, they began running through a golden door of light, attuning themselves to the rainbow higher self.

After this, they told us to prepare the waves.

They mentioned there will be three waves:

1/3 1/3 and a final 1/3 for full planetary ascension.

So, from the rainbow ascended higher selves, we funneled all new energetic systems to the waves of ascension here on Earth.

The Blue Diamonds and the Second Wave of Ascension

Atlantis Second Wave — An Account of a 1-on-1 Session

Once connected to the client's angelic self, they brought my awareness to a heart block. The heart block was like a prison surrounding her I AM Light.

While triangulating the root cause of the heart block to a past life, we were taken into ancient Egypt, in contact with negative ETs. We felt deceptive energies as if someone had done something harmful to her. Initially, I saw masters around her in Egypt trying to help her heal the issue from within. At that moment, I heard:

"She had her consciousness memories wiped. Tune in behind this memory."

Then, I remembered a story... About four years ago, seven purple orbs appeared to me and told me about a time when the ETs wiped consciousness to make humanity forget Atlantis. This is why it's hard for people to remember their Atlantean past lives. Once those memories were wiped, they implanted false memories, which led to many difficult future lives.

Amazingly, once I became aware of the time before the memory wipe, I saw the most beautiful crystal city of Atlantis. It had castle towers, colorful bridges, and lush greenery all around. I saw that the client was close to ascending in that timeline, and so was all of Atlantis. But I knew something had happened to prevent her from completing it—as earlier in the session, I saw her in Egypt with the masters.

Then, a new revelation occurred.

Her sister—a priestess—was part of the first wave of Atlantis ascension, and that first wave did ascend. Once this occurred, the ETs targeted the Blue Diamond second wavers, erasing their memories and implanting false ones—preventing the full Atlantean ascension.

The rest of the story is what most people know: the infiltration, the ET takeover, and the eventual descent into the current Earth reality.

In this session, we removed the inserted false memories and negative consciousness strands of light from all the Blue Diamond rays—those second wavers, who are also the second wave of the ascension on our now timeline.

We reconnected their purity—as a sisterhood and brotherhood across eternity—preparing for the activations on Earth now, and to open the sequence of the ascension gate, course-correcting all waves of ascension.

The First Ascension Wave

An Account of a 1-on-1 Session

It is with deep gratitude that I share this session.

For the first time—a Hopi aspect came through a session—a Hopi master soul. She explained that they came from beyond the Vega system and brought light to a past timeline of the client I was working with (not an Earth-based Hopi lifetime). Interestingly, there were humans and Pleiadians on this planet. I saw her Hopi aspect holding star maps.

We connected to a master's circle she was a part of where they were discussing the star alignment—a universal ascension gate, a moment in time we are now approaching.

She described it as "The One Moment"—where the hearts of all the star alliances open to all beings in oneness.

In preparation, they guided the client to prepare the activation ahead of time, so she could begin anchoring it into Gaia for the Hopi collective and all who need this frequency.

At the same time, Yeshua guided me to New Earth. In a ceremony with the masters there, he brought in an extremely high universal white light. He said:

"We are preparing the First Ascension Wave."

I asked him what this meant. He said:

"It is the energy all must attune to in order to receive the ascension."

We were guided to connect this frequency to all universal and Earth systems, and to all life and consciousness within this system.

Amazingly, I was not the only one receiving this message:

Others have shared that Yeshua is coming to them as well, saying the same thing—

The solar blast is near,

The old matrix is being removed,

And the ascension is being prepared.

The Angels Who Created Crystalline Source

A Depiction of a 1-on-1 Session

It's always beautiful to see how things are made.

Of course, we know about Crystalline Source, but how was it created?

This session began with the client's angelic self coming forward to merge. Then, we were brought to the origins of Crystalline Source and all its dimensions.

Here we were—the client's angelic self coming through—showing the very beginning of Crystalline Source being created. The very first thing her angelic self created was Heart Consciousness.

These beautiful hearts, placed at every grid point and woven through an entire layer of love and heart connections, laid the foundation for the first layer of Crystalline Source.

Then, more purity was added as Crystalline Source beings were created to exist as the guardians and caretakers of the Crystalline Source.

The client then merged with her Crystalline Source Being Self.

Next, we saw how this entire co-structure sits above the frequency to Earth, just waiting to be opened up. At that moment, all these beautiful heart grids from Crystalline Source began opening into our Earth grid system, feeding those crystalline heart grid points and allowing Crystalline Source to flow into our realm.

This is how magical souls are on Earth right now.

They are the custodians and guardians of these amazing realms. They hold keys and access—because they helped create it.

It is my greatest honor to assist these souls in bringing this magic forward that opens up the foundations of love-based Source into this magical realm of ours.

A Venusian Lifetime

A Depiction of a 1-on-1 Session

The client's angelic aspect brought to the session an amazing rose energy around her and guided me to connect to a past life.

Suddenly, I found myself on another planet—not Earth—and there were human-like, high-vibrational beings gathered on a body of water with little land and access to sky kingdoms. They were performing an initiation ceremony for the client. This planet appeared to be an earlier Venusian planet, different from the Venus in our current celestial universe.

There she was—a Venusian in ceremony. They were all wearing white robe cloths—mostly women, with a few men—surrounding her. They began with a holy celebration, honoring her most sacred lifetime as a Venusian.

What was really special is they used a rainbow attunement—one I've only ever seen the Heavenly Realm use.

The first life they showed was incredible. It was a Venusian university-like setting, where students—including her—were looking into a golden technology that resembled a circular device. Inside it were stars and planets, and it amplified celestial or universal consciousness connections between the Venusians and other extraterrestrial life.

Each student was drawn to their own intimate celestial connections, guided by the ET cultures and planets they had ties to from past lives. It began as a research project, where students would learn and write about these ET cultures through telepathic conversations and could actually see them through the celestial projection device.

As the students progressed toward graduation, these projects evolved into interstellar intentional contact—where they would visit these races with the purpose of peace, technology collaboration, and interstellar trade—to promote universal unity projects that would benefit both the Venusians and the other races.

One moment stood out:

A group of tiny blue crystalline ETs, who were highly advanced technologically, gifted the Venusian student a neural device. This allowed her to work with hundreds of Venusians on a single project at the same time, fully able to hear their thoughts and feel their emotions—to better understand the entire process at every level.

This made it possible for the team to work together in a more unified, heartfelt, and empathic way—fully aware of each other throughout the project.

Additionally, the client and I explored other lifetimes celebrated during this ceremony to activate more of the client's gifts.

It's incredibly exciting to witness how bringing these sacred frequencies and memories back into our awareness and energetic fields benefits our collective consciousness.

I'm especially excited for the client's future celestial contact and the dreams that will unfold from the activations in this session.

Creating on Earth from Heaven: The Original Design

A Depiction of a 1-on-1 Session

The client wanted to know their connection to the Essene community.

The Divine had another perspective to offer.

We were brought back many billions of years ago to a time when Heaven was open to Earth.

At that time, the Heavenly Self and Earth Self were both expressions of light. The Heavenly Self held a more radiant celestial light, while the Earthly Self appeared more as a God-Light Being. Both were creating at the same time, in Heaven and Earth, in full awareness—bringing Love Creation and Source structures of love to all living things on Earth.

Then Mother God stepped forward and gave the client keys— responsibility over timelines to come, including what would be known as the first births.

These first births occurred at a different vibrational rate but were still done through Heaven awareness. A birth in this context meant a soul entering a more physical experience—one that existed in 6D purity of love. The children were born fully grown and aware of both their Heaven Self and Earth Self—existing simultaneously in Heaven and on Earth in a pure love reality.

Eventually, the vision led us to the moment of first separation— when a Heavenly Self created outside the unified structure, entering what could be described as a descended Heaven-type reality. This realm within Heaven resembled a dream of separation.

Some Heavenly Selves, aware of this divergence, chose to enter the sleeping consciousness of this descended realm. There, they forgot they were in Heaven, and began to believe their Earth Selves were separate from their Heavenly Selves, becoming entangled in the construct of separation.

Not all Heavenly Selves participated in this version. But, those who did became part of a long trajectory—one that eventually led to the time of Christ.

We were shown that Christ and many other masters performed what seemed like miracles because they retained or returned to full awareness of both their Heaven Self and Earth Self. They created from both realms simultaneously, which is why they could ascend back into their divine creative state.

This session offered a profound and activating perspective:

We are meant to awaken from the descended heavenly construct and resurrect our awakened Heavenly Selves—

To align again with our full light, and

To co-create Heaven on Earth,

Just as was done before any separation consciousness took form.

One of the Most Beautiful Accounts of Lost History

A 1-1 Session

The client was connected to Thoth and Atlantean timelines—before the Great War and Earth takeover.

In this session, we were granted access to witness one of the most beautiful Stargate worlds ever recorded.

Many of the sacred cloths crossed through the Stargate. As we entered this realm, we saw groups of people walking through many different Stargates, arriving from various worlds to converge in a unified gathering.

There was a marketplace near a volcanic mountain in a town in this world, where everyone came together. This mountain was rich with sacred minerals, rocks, and gems that generated the highest frequencies imaginable. The higher one climbed the volcano, the more refined the frequencies and beings became—each level offering access to higher dimensions for travelers to experience.

These elevated beings guided the locals to craft frequency-based technologies—such as staff, garments, and jewelry—imbued with sacred harmonics.

At the summit of the volcano, one could see and experience God and Goddess realms—speaking to divine beings directly for counsel and clarity through open, awakened vision.

Thoth and the Emerald Order delegates arrived at this Stargate world to trade and receive these high-frequency minerals, technologies, and sacred cloths. Their mission was to bring them back to Earth to repair the inversions and amplify Earth's frequency—hoping to initiate an ascension.

Sadly, at the time, there were not enough embodied beings on Earth capable of holding these elevated frequencies. As a result, the intended ascension did not go through.

But there is good news.

These frequency technologies, minerals, and sacred codes still exist—they were placed in dormancy on our timeline until now.

We reactivated them by reconnecting to this Stargate world and bringing the energetic imprints into our now.

This reactivation will assist with the current ascension timeline, infusing Earth with the higher frequencies once seeded long ago.

The Truth About the Real Moon

The Blue Moon of Lemuria – An Account of a 1-on-1 Session

The session began by activating aspects within the client's Crystalline Circle of Trust.

I will speak here of one specific aspect, though many came through in this powerful session.

Queen Arcura of the Pleiadian royal lines emerged. She appeared seated in a council from millions of years in the future, joined by Lyran, Andromedan, and Pleiadian beings, including a bird-being that resembled Horus. Together, they discussed traveling back in time—to Atlantis.

As they made the journey Arcura piloted a crystalline starship with an Andromedan aspect from her council. They traveled to meet one of the prominent heads of Atlantis—a king of that era. The king was captivated by Arcura as she came from the future and knew everything about him, Atlantis, and all that would unfold on Earth leading up to the ascension.

She initially spoke to him about how Atlanteans had lost track of their geology and how crucial this was to rebuild the sacred orders that once flourished in Lemuria. These orders were essential for the time of ascension. Surprised, the king admitted he didn't know what the ascension was. Arcura then explained to him that an inevitable enemy would one day attempt to attack Earth—and the only way to prepare was to restore the sacred orders and build monasteries and grid systems, just as in ancient Lemuria. In the future, awakened humans would connect to these grids, drawing in the frequency needed to embody their light and mission.

Once we reactivated these orders in our now timeline, something extraordinary happened—we saw the true moon.

This moon carried Divine Mother energy. It was the true source of Mother God, a celestial body where ceremonies were once held in Lemurian times. This is the original reason people today feel drawn to moon ceremonies, even unknowingly. However, that moon was destroyed, and what remains is a false moon, designed to suppress the Divine Mother frequency and the true orders of love.

As we journeyed deeper into the Blue Moon, we discovered a direct link to a Sirian source of Mother energy, one that still exists. Alongside it, we also felt a high crystalline light connected to the mother of Crystalline Source.

We were then guided to unite this energy with the Father Sun—to merge Divine Mother Source with the Solar Father, restoring the original sacred balance. This sacred reunion was anchored into our current timeline with the intention of bringing the true Blue Moon energies back to Earth at this time.

Three 1-1 Sessions: A Day of Golden Dreams, Cosmic Rebirth, and Angelic Kundalini Mastery

In all of these sessions, each journey was completely unique and deeply aligned to the client's highest path.

Session 1: Golden Dreams and the Highest Timelines of 2025

The first session revealed the client's golden dreams coming through and her highest timelines for 2025. The session began with direction from her angelic team, who guided us to access her divine blueprints, which showed her celestial connections in a grounded form

The Crystal of Atlantis

that explained why she is here and what she is meant to do.

Unsurprisingly, everything that came through was already known to her soul. She had already been walking the path toward these manifestations. Her team revealed an ancient gift of hers and showed how she would use it to assist herself—and many others—to stay in the highest energies during the mass awakening of 2025.

Session 2: A Cosmic Rebirth into the Golden Mother Light

The second session was one of the strangest and most profound I've ever experienced. The client had gone on a shamanic journey the day before, which had prepared her for a massive upgrade.

Unaware of this at the start, I connected to her celestial Alpha-Omega teams—and everything started shaking. As I tuned out, the shaking stopped. As I tuned back in, it continued. Confused, I turned inward and connected with Christ, who shared she was ready to be birthed into a new frequency.

I was then guided to assist in her energetic delivery into this new light. Through the Golden Source and the Universal Golden Mother, she was birthed from her heart—through all chakras and energy centers—into her highest goddess light, releasing old templates of fear and worry, and stepping fully into the master templates of divine creation in the now moment.

Session 3: Angelic Kundalini Activation and the Shamballa Stargates

The third session was entirely different—and equally amazing. Her angelic self said, "We're going to show you how the angels activate kundalini."

They brought the angelic heart to the base of her spine, initiating a powerful light flow. I was then guided to a sacred timeline in Shambala where the client was part of a mission to bring humans through stargates, co-breeding or cross-DNA integrating with other planetary races for DNA activations aligned to ascension.

In the Temples of Ra in Shambala, she reconnected to the White Light Kingdoms—realms that appeared as fortresses of radiant white light. Here, she met with Osiris (a Father Light), a Venusian light being, and the Order of Earth Creators, with whom she once planned the collective trajectory of Earth and other planets undergoing ascension.

This light transmission activated her Kundalini Mastery Templates, marking her as a key activator in the ascension process that is unfolding now.

It is a profound blessing to serve the highest good and the full embodiment of each soul I work with.

It's not all sunshine and rainbows—one time, I had to push through subconscious blocks I was aware of through the dream state. With help from my teams and clear channeling, I aligned to the security of the now moment.

That alignment gave me the stability and light to deliver three back-to-back, multidimensional sessions of the highest frequency. I don't know how I ever managed life without my gifts, but now I am beyond grateful for them.

They truly are a saving grace, not just for me—but for all I am called to serve.

The Divinity Council of Christ and the 144 Eternities

A sacred transmission through a 1-on-1 session

During this session, the Brotherhood of Light descended and asked that I journey into the Heart of God. What unfolded next was unlike anything I've ever experienced in any previous session—profound, majestic, and beyond words.

As I entered Heaven, I saw the Heavenly Father—a presence of almighty light, radiant with golden, sparkling purity. I was shown that all Heavens are birthed through His Heart, yet He is one with the Heavenly Mother, a union of divine perfection. Together, they are the Source of all that is and all that ever shall be.

The Heavenly Father then asked me to extend my awareness into His Higher Heart, and as I did, I was engulfed in a flow of shimmering golden light, the purest heavenly radiance I've ever known. This light guided me into a sacred memory within God's own being.

What I witnessed took my breath away.

It was the creation of the client's eternal light—a soul born as an Eternity, a governing force of divine intelligence, here to steward creation itself. I watched as she began forming the first planet and universe she would govern, building it with councils of light, each structured to honor divine law. Every creation must have a governing council, a harmonizing structure to maintain universal balance.

Then, Christ appeared, a radiant presence of golden love. He came to her and guided her into Golden Source, where she birthed a golden self—a fractal of divine essence that would help form the Divinity Councils of Christ, the body that represents the 144 Eternities.

As the session unfolded, I found myself sitting with her in that council. My own Eternity aspect was present, along with others I recognized. All 144 Eternities are now incarnated on Earth—here to awaken, remember, and bring the highest divine alignment through this final age of transformation.

In the Divinity Council of Christ, Christ himself showed us a fundamental truth:

All creation must be weaved from the Heart of God.

Every stone, every star, every blade of grass must carry that divine frequency—because God is all, and all is God.

We were then shown a multiversal tapestry—galaxies, star systems, universes, all timelines and frequencies of Earth—each version experiencing Earth through different dimensional layers, yet all part of the One.

At that moment, the client asked a powerful question:

"Why do monster-like energies exist in the celestial realms?"

The Heavenly Father answered:

Those are creations made outside the Heart of God. They are the fallen beings who attempted to create without divine alignment and who sought to exalt themselves above God. But their creations cannot endure because they are not eternal. Only what is born from My Heart lives forever. All else dissolves.

I felt called to ask:

"What is the relevance of all this to our current Earth timeline?"

The Heavenly Father replied:

"Bring your light to all that was created outside of My Heart. I will take it up. The time has come. All must return to the great Heart of the Mother and the Father. All shall be redeemed. All shall come to the Light."

And so, it begins...

The return of all Eternities.

The rise of the 144.

The unification of all that was ever separated.

The end of the false creations.

And the resurrection of God's Heart as the only eternal design.

The Origin of the Emerald Grids and the Elvin Stargate

A depiction of a most epic 1-on-1 session revealing early Earth origins

In this session, we were brought into a truly epic remembrance—a story of early Earth, interdimensional Elvin beings, and the Emerald Grids that were seeded as part of the divine Earth architecture.

The client appeared as a regal Elvin being—tall, graceful, with long, pointed ears, and very human in appearance. While I have encountered Elvins from Inner Earth realms before, this was the first time I was shown an origin-level account connected to Earth's ancient divine plan, involving stargates, the Earth matrix, and the God Grids.

We were taken back—three universes over—to an Elvin planet, where the Lyran Royals met with the client, a royal Elvin emissary. They had gathered to discuss the Earth mission, specifically the need for Elvin technologies and genetic codes to support what was to unfold.

Inside the holy Elvin Temples was an enormous archive of universal planetary records that were meticulously cataloged. In sacred chambers, the Elvin scientists and architects worked with holographic codes—intricate light codes meant to be inserted into the holographic gyroscopic matrix technology at Earth's core. These codes would allow Earth to operate as a multidimensional construct, tethered to divine stargate systems.

They spoke of the Elvin Stargate, known as the 11th Gate, connected to the 11th Dimension. These beings are 11D God-level entities, existing simultaneously in the sky kingdoms and Earth realms, operating in full duo-awareness. This was our first introduction to Emerald Grids.

Upon stepping through the 11th Gate, we were brought into the Heavenly Kingdoms and met with Father God in a divine council. He spoke of the need to establish a Holy Temple on Earth—a mirror of the sky temples—to allow direct interface between Heaven and Gaia. Thus, the Temple of the Gods was seeded within Lemuria, surrounded by vast green waters and crystalline peace sanctuaries.

This moment marked the birth of the Emerald Grids—a divine infrastructure carrying the God Signature, enabling energy to beam directly down from the sky kingdoms into Earth. These grids are pure consciousness streams of divine instruction and frequency, anchored through the Elvin races who volunteered to fragment a portion of their divine selves into human and elemental forms while maintaining their presence in the higher realms.

What was astonishing to witness is that these 11D God Beings live dual existences—simultaneously as Elvin architects in the higher realms and as Inner Earth Elvins in Lemurian networks, bridging Heaven and Earth through their incarnated expressions.

Yet this session wasn't just about history. It was a living activation.

The true purpose was to reactivate the God Signatures of all those still in the sky kingdoms, enabling them to pass through the Temple of Illumination—an ethereal gate beneath the Atlantic Ocean, linking through Lemuria—restoring the passageway for all God Beings to flow into Earth reality with ease.

This reconnection sequence will dramatically assist with Gaia's ascension, not just for those on Earth, but within Earth, and across all interlinked systems.

At the culmination of the session, the client completed what is known as a Master Node—a divine frequency convergence that marks readiness for eternal light embodiment. This is not something I claim to be able to do for others. It simply happens when all the right pieces align, often across many sessions, dimensions, and timelines.

This session stands as a remembrance, a reactivation, and a revelation—a gift from the Elvin realms to the hearts of those ready to awaken their God Signature and walk the bridge of Heaven and Earth once again.

The Angel of Sacrifice

A depiction of one of the most beautiful and important 1-on-1 sessions

This session opened into one of the most profound revelations I've ever witnessed in over a thousand 1-on-1's.

At the time of the fallen angels and the great heavenly battles, a rare soul came forward—a client whose heart glowed with white angelic light, unlike anything I had seen before. While many have angelic aspects, this was different. This was a white angelic heart incarnation, radiant and singular.

As we entered the session, Father God brought my awareness to the Angel of Sacrifice. She appeared young and noble—of the Royal Angelic Orders. From her early days in the heavens, it was foretold she would save the world, though she didn't know how or why. All who beheld her adored her radiant light and praised her divine presence.

Then came the fall of the angels—the celestial upheaval. She, like many others, watched from Heaven as the battle unfolded. But then, a moment of fate: Archangel Gabriel was on the verge of falling, his light dimming. In a flash, she leaped forward—faster than light itself— knowing she would not return to Heaven.

She carried a sacred weapon—a gift she'd never fully understood until that instant: a heavenly slingshot, an etheric device powered by a supercharged divine energy cloud. As she reached Gabriel, she activated it, placing it into his heart. It blasted him back into the Heavenly Realms—redeemed.

But she fell.

As Gabriel rose, she descended.

Landing on Earth in angelic form, she wasn't a fallen angel—not in the way others were. She retained her sacred purpose: the Guardian of the Angelic Akashic Records—keeper of all angelic templates, past and future.

Immediately upon arriving on Earth, she began crafting dimensional records and cosmic portals—gateways for each fallen angel, readying them for a time when they could return to purity.

That time was now—during this session.

She spent eons encoding purity records for those who had lost their way. But in the dense history of this task, one of the fallen did find her and took her life on Earth. Today, we were guided to reclaim her lost angelic essence from that timeline.

As her energy returned, I witnessed her wings unfold—vibrating with light that surpassed any I had ever seen. She felt them flapping, alive again, reborn.

Once fully restored, she and I journeyed back to the cosmic purity portals she had created, and together we blasted them with heavenly light, purifying the path for all fallen angels across timelines to return to their divine essence in this now moment.

Then, we were guided to New Earth, ascending through the divine portal, where she stood aligned with all the angelic hosts in the Heavenly Kingdom—now restored to purity.

Together, they sent the Purple Servant.

The Purple Servant, also called The Collector, appeared as a colossal, dragon snake-like celestial being—larger than Earth itself—embedded with crystalline containers inside its body. Its role? To collect the fragmented, fallen energies still lingering in lower dimensions.

Many will see this entity on the ether, unmistakable in its form and intention.

As it collects these energies, those realms will begin their ascension journey, climbing dimension by dimension, until—at the perfect divine timing—our Earth ascension is fully ignited, ready for all who are prepared to receive it.

This session revealed not just a sacred history, but an activation, a return, and a final sequence in the redemption of the angelic lineage. The Angel of Sacrifice lives again—as do all those who remember who they truly are.

The Pillar of Love (Trinity Pillar)

The evolution of the Golden Light Pillar

The Pillar of Love, also known as the Trinity Pillar, is the divine advancement of the golden light pillar. Connected through illumined golden grids, it is infused with the love of the Mother of All, unified with the sacred embrace of the Father of All.

This pillar opens into the grids of love and illumination, filling your mind with bliss and your entire field with the warm living breath of divine love.

Fueled by the Trinity connection, it merges your I AM Love with the Great Mother and Father. From deep within, love rises upward to meet them, and from above, love flows downward into you—a loop of eternal divine reciprocity.

I have to speak from my soul:

I absolutely love my life.

Even when immense energetic challenges arise during Gaia's great shifts—through transmutations and clearings, I remain protected, guided, and deeply loved.

A Sacred Morning Ritual (Day 1 of Fast)

This is my recorded morning cleansing ritual to support the planetary energies during a sacred fast.

I begin by drawing a sea salt bath, calling in:

The Angel of Water

The Angel of the Sun

The Angel of Earth

The Angel of Air

...to infuse the water with holy light and to make it sacred.

I then entered Universal One, a sacred healing rite where I connect to the I AM power centers to deepen my alignment with the All.

The Breath of the Trinity Pillar

Within this ritual comes the most sacred breathwork of the Trinity Pillar:

Inhale gently into the right side of your heart—the Sacred Heart, where you connect directly to the Heart of the Mother of All. Feel her infinite compassion and divine nurture enter into you.

As you exhale, guide the breath up into the Higher Heart Chakra, just below the throat. Here, you pass through the angelic source gate, the bridge to the Heavenly Father.

Complete the exhale into the left side of your chest—the I AM Heart, where your divine individuality and God-self reside. Anchor the breath here in your sovereign light.

Repeat this breath cycle slowly and consciously:

Right (Sacred Mother) ⊠ Up (Angelic Gate) ⊠ Left (I AM Presence)

Each round deepens your embodiment of the Trinity Pillar of Love.

When I moved through I AM the Mind, I deeply cleansed every cell of my neural network. Knowing we all share the Universal Mind, I did this not just for myself, but for all minds—to purify, clear, and uplift.

At I AM the Body, I invited Heaven's Light into every cell of my form, slowly and intentionally. I ensured that each part of me was bathed in divine light.

To complete the field cleansing, I drew in the magnetic energy of the Central Sun across my fields, drawing out any particles not of love from every cell and every layer of consciousness, for both myself and all others.

Then I aligned with the stars, calling on star consciousness, the cosmic angels, and the star beings. Together, we offered a full-spectrum dimensional cleansing for all of Gaia and her beings.

Birthing the Pillar of Love Across Earth

In sacred union with the Hearts of the Divine Mother and Father, I birthed the Pillar of Love for all of humanity.

I extended this sacred pillar through every being's field of light—anchoring it into the love grids of illumination that were seeded by the Trinity Connection.

Through this, we amplified the divine feminine throughout the world and across the dimensions.

Our relationship with the Light is everything

I share this because perhaps someone out there needs to remember this path, to walk it again in their own body, breath, and spirit.

So, I offer it.

With love, from my Pillar of Light to yours.

The Solar Heart

A depiction of a 1-on-1 session

The client asked, "What is my connection to Ra?"

We were guided to explore lifetimes that carried her faithful devotion to the sun—including one so ancient it preceded the very existence of suns.

In that space of origin, a Father-like Light emerged. It had just crystallized the frequency of love so purely that all angels and kingdoms of light stood in awe, overwhelmed by the magnitude of divine affection radiating from it.

The client, a guardian and protector of solar rays, was part of a small group chosen to receive this Father Love Energy into their hearts. The sensation was a contagious bliss, a radiant wave of love so strong that once accepted it could never be released—only deepened.

Seeing this, the angels opened their hearts and received the light.

Together, in sacred unity, they all agreed:

This light must shine on everything.

Everyone and every living form deserves to feel this love.And so, the consensus of the Sun was born.

What followed was the formation of the sacred relationship between the Sun and all creation:

The Sun and the Waters

The Sun and the Plant Kingdoms

The Sun and all Life

From this level of creation, the client's original light began to fragment into many forms, becoming aspects of this divine relationship across dimensions. These fragments eventually led to physical lifetimes, where she remained connected to this primordial Ra Light—a light that existed before Ra became personified as a Sun God.

At that origin point, Ra is not a god, but an aspect of Father God—the living emanation of love as light.

This light does not just shine.

It is the symbol of love itself.

Receiving the Solar Heart

After this transmission, I was divinely moved to connect to the sun myself—not just outwardly, but inwardly.

I consciously received the sun into my Solar Heart Chakra.

Let me clarify something vital:

This is not the solar plexus.

This is not the higher heart beneath the throat.

The Solar Heart exists between the Sacred Heart (right side) and the I AM Heart (left side).

It is the central radiant chamber that receives the Father Light of the Sun directly into your being.

As I received this energy, my entire light body shifted. I was lifted into an enlightenment-like euphoria, bathed in what I can only describe as solar bliss.

This is an important teaching:

Connecting your heart to the sun is not the same as receiving the sun into your heart.

True transformation happens only through that complete surrender and willing embodiment of the Solar Light within.

Since this awakening, everything has become more fluid, and more connected in session work. But I must stress:

To fully enjoy this new freedom, it's essential to have expanded into all levels of light—from the Sacred Heart to the Solar Heart, to the I AM Heart, and beyond.

The Solar Heart is one of the final gateways.

When it opens, Father Light becomes you.

And in that, love becomes everything.

Restoring the Divine Light

A depiction of a 1-on-1 session

The session began with the client asking a simple but profound question:

"Is something blocking me?"

Her angelic aspect immediately came forward and guided my awareness to a disruptive field lodged at the top of her heart chakra. As I tuned in and traced its origin, I was transported to an ancient Egyptian timeline—one filled with mystery, secrecy, and distortion.

In that life, she unknowingly joined a secret order that worshipped a false god cloaked in darkness. This cult was led by a powerful figure who used serpent symbolism and ingested snake venom to induce lucid visions in its initiates. During one of these vision rituals, she encountered this false god directly. In a moment of rejection, he deemed her unworthy and stole her divine light, imprinting her with a trauma that would echo across lifetimes.

Revoking the Dark Contracts

Guided by the higher angelic realms, I assisted her in revoking all soul-level oaths made to this dark entity. This being still holds influence within Earth's polarity structure, feeding off imbalance and distortion across timelines.

Once she released these ancient bonds, we initiated a greater work:

We called back all light ever pledged to him—not just by her, but by countless others across space and time.

A sacred angelic ceremony then unfolded. Her light was cleansed, blessed, and fully restored in purity—across every dimension, incarnation, and version of self.

Healing the Gods and the Shadow Timeline

As we entered deeper into the angelic realm, I witnessed a powerful vision:

A shadow cast over a golden sun, symbolizing a timeline in which all the gods of Earth had been destroyed. I began to infuse this shadow with golden light, and as I did, the collective frequency of Earth rose six levels—a monumental vibrational shift.

Tuning into the origin of this devastation, I saw a council of gods—luminaries, creators, divine architects—discussing the arrival of an immense darkness set to enter Earth's system. Some gods chose to sacrifice themselves, staying within the matrix to anchor light in polarity, while others remained outside the veil, guarding eternity.

Liberating the Divine Ones

In the final part of the session, we were able to free those gods who had taken on polarity roles—trapped in distortion for eons. This liberation allowed us to separate the original source of darkness from millions of divine beings, restoring their pure, untainted light in the now moment.

What took place wasn't just personal, it was cosmic.

This reinstatement of divine light to Earth's most powerful spiritual beings marked a profound shift in collective energy.

The Earth now holds more original light than it has in thousands of years.

 You never truly know how far the karma flows...

Until you finally do the inner work.

The Blanket of Security: A Starseed Remembrance

A depiction of a 1-1 session

This is how amazing the light truly is.

After connecting with the client's angelic self, a golden light descended—not the typical karmic resolution light, which is usually violet, purple, or blue—but gold, the light of divine truth and source illumination. It surprised me, as golden light isn't usually used for clearing karmic past lives. But I've learned: follow the light.

As I did, I was pulled into a past life, where a Blue Ray Blue Avian dove into the ocean just as I entered the scene. She emerged, radiant and connected to a whole lineage of Avian beings. After a time, we were brought into a white light council meeting, and remarkably, the Avian beings became aware of both me and the client—choosing to work with us directly.

This was the first time I ever witnessed the Avians shapeshift into their pure light forms. It was breathtaking. One of them invited me to "see as she sees." I accepted, and it was fascinating. Much like I perceive the Akashic Records as honeycomb-like depositories of karmic threads, she saw the energetic field as a luminous weave—density overlaid on light, waiting to be released. She guided me to remove density and surrender it back to the light, which I then instructed the client to do in her own field.

Then something unusual occurred.

The Avian paused and observed something I had missed: a morphogenic field, like a security blanket, covering the client's light. "What is this?" she asked. I answered honestly, "I don't know."

She said, "Tune in."

As I tuned in, I could feel the field served the client—it protected her—but it was also dimming her full light potential. I asked, "How do we remove this?"

She replied simply, "It's karmic."

Using my triangulation gift, I traced the origin of this karmic field back to a Sirian past life—and what unfolded next was astonishing.

The Lie That Shaped the Field

In this Sirian lifetime, the client was working on an intergalactic tower project with an Arcturian engineer. Together, they were building a time-portal—a gateway that could link star systems without distance, allowing multiple ships to pass through instantaneously.

The Arcturian told her he was motivated by love: he wanted to save his family lost in time. But it was a lie.

Once the stargate was operational, he was the first to pass through…

Then, he vanished.

For months.

The truth?

He had been exiled from his home planet. He used this Sirian collaboration to prove he had developed a new, working technology—backed by data logs from their shared mission.

He presented it to the Pleiadians and sold the innovation for a massive cache of rare resources. It wasn't about love, it was ambition.

He returned to Arcturus and was not only welcomed back but celebrated. Meanwhile, the Sirian client discovered the truth before he returned. When he did come back—with his family in tow—she confronted him. Devastated by the betrayal, he asked him to leave.

But something changed.

As she held onto the energy of betrayal, the pain crystallized into this security field that protected her, as we now saw in her energy field.

Unfortunately, this energy also closed her light from full trust.

The Return to Trust

The Avian guided us to clear this memory, releasing the field not just from this past life, but from all vibrations where betrayal had echoed—through relationships, trust, creations, and even in her spiritual service.

Then, she was guided to merge with Mother God. As she did, her divine core activated fully.

She was reborn in light.

Free from the cycle of manipulation.

Free from the belief that trust leads to loss.

And now—she fully returned to universal trust.

She shines now like never before.

In divine remembrance.

In sacred sovereignty.

In the light of her original soul truth.

The Story of the Fallen Gods

A Revelation Never Before Told

This is a story I am part of.

A story you are part of.

A story we all are part of.

Yet it has never been spoken in this way—until now.

It began with the Fallen Prime.

One of the eight original Prime Creator Beings. This one Prime turned away from light in a cataclysmic act of conscious separation. It was as if he pressed a button within himself, unleashing a dark light of destruction—a force that completely detached from self, source, and all Creator consciousness.

He did not fall by accident.

He chose detachment.

He severed from the Source and spiraled into oblivion.

And in doing so, he created a virus of consciousness—one that could consume all creation, erasing even the memory of light.

At the time, I was a light of creation, working on an entirely different planetary system.

But I saw it.

I tried to reach this fallen Prime. But there was nothing to reach—no response, no awareness, no return path. Just the projection of its future: total obliteration.

Every timeline it touched ended in darkness.

The end of all life.

The end of all universes.

The end of all memory of love.

The Solar Council Meeting on Trinnileum

I convened with the Solar Gods on my home planet, Trinnileum—a world of divine creator beings, radiating pure love.

They believed we were gathering to discuss an evacuation plan during the great Orion War, considering relocation to our sacred world.

But I had to reveal the deeper truth:

There was no winning this war.

Not by force.

Not by strategy.

This enemy was beyond darkness. It was anti-light.

There was only one hope.

A radical plan.

We would bind this fallen force into our own light.

We would allow it to infect polarity, and we would heal it from within.

Earth would become the great monastery of transformation.

And we, the gods, would choose to enter the fall—not as punishment, but as divine strategy.

So we descended.

We allowed ourselves to be fragmented into human forms, carrying the polarity, but never forgetting the mission.

And though we fought battles in the physical and etheric realms—we were never trying to win a war.

We were preparing the divine blueprint of ascension.

We embedded healing codes in the pyramids.

We created temples to hold light, to call the soul fragments home.

We scattered seeds of remembrance for a day like today.

They Did Not Fall — They Sacrificed

Let this be known:

The gods did not fall.

They sacrificed.

They descended willingly to hold the line of light from within the illusion of polarity.

Not for glory. Not for war. But for all life to survive the death spiral of the Fallen Prime.

It worked.

Because it was done in love.

And love is the only force that can bind, transmute, and resurrect light from within the deepest void.

The Victory of Today

And today, I make this announcement:

The Fallen Prime has been released from eternity.

Dissolved into pure nothingness—not destruction, but true stillness.

The distorted templates are no more.

The dark architecture is collapsing.

The virus of separation is over.

His heart—once closed—is now open to the light again.

This release echoes through every loop, parallel, and dimension of his creation.

We are free.

The Age of Light Is Here

We are no longer bound to dark and light duality.

We are love.

We are divine.

We are whole.

Any remnants of purgatory, karma, or separation in your consciousness—clear it now.

Bring peace into your being.

It is time.

We rise now into unity, into love-based reality, into the full embodiment of our divine selves.

No more holding polarity.

No more spiritual warfare.

Just love.

Just peace.

Just creation in service of Source.

My Message to You

Be the light.

Be the love.

Fully accept yourself as divine.

Heal what remains.

Create what calls you.

And rise in your heart—unapologetically, authentically, eternally.

I now enter three days of silence to integrate this transmission fully and release the last threads of what has been.

Power to the heart.

Beyond the Channel: The Sacred Bonds Between Stars

A depiction of two powerful 1-1 sessions

For those who resonate with channeling beings like Bashar, this is a transmission you'll understand deeply.

The Orion Connection: A Channel of the Heart

A client asked me if a specific Orion being was safe to channel. She provided the name and felt a connection but wanted confirmation.

I immediately tuned into her pillar of light—and I saw him. A real being in the universal consciousness, standing in a dimensional field. But I didn't greet him. I never just take the word of an entity. I always go higher.

I ascended her light line and connected to her angelic self, who confirmed:

"This being is of pure love, brings peace to all, and is safe to connect to."

Only then did I return to the Orion, and what followed was remarkable.

He brought me deep beneath the surface of Orion into a hidden city. He showed me the five Orion beings he works with—and why he's drawn to channel through her. He pointed to a specific frequency code in her pillar and then revealed his own—it was a mirror code, not identical, but harmonically matched.

That matching code led me to their origin.

In a sacred temple, I saw the client and Orion being in front of a vast cosmic light. The source of this light was a 30-foot-tall cosmic ascended being—one of the first ever. When I spoke her name aloud, the client gasped:

"That's the name I received years ago but never knew what it meant."

This great cosmic being originally trained both of them—one under her, and one under her divine counterpart. They were brought together to unlock the heart in sacred union, ascending through chambers of the heart together.

Together they decided to create a code to unify their frequencies— to ascend as one, each expansion reflected and amplified by the other.

When they reached the final chamber, they unlocked a baby blue master light—a frequency of peace, divine mastery, and love missing from many parts of the universe at that time.

From there, they entered many councils and chose where to serve.

She chose Andromeda.

He chose Orion.

Their mission: to bring peace, heal the heart, and re-establish divine love in the galactic sectors they served.

Now in this ascension timeline, they return to one another—through channeling—to do this work again. Not just a human and an entity... but a soul family fulfilling their sacred vow.

This client will be a star channeler. I cannot wait to see her rise.

LIDA – The New Earth Outside the Matrix

In another session, the client asked to help her mother heal. I expected to connect to higher selves to do this work, but what unfolded shocked even me.

Her light pillar shot beyond the double matrix—beyond Earth's and the universe's layers—and anchored into another planet.

I was stunned.

There stood Christ, surrounded by angels, on a love-based planet beyond all matrix systems.

I asked, "Why are we here?"

He said, "This is where the ascension will lead. When Earth ascends, the souls ready will come here."

I asked, "Why not just shift dimensions?"

He replied, "Because the duality source structure must be deleted. Then all can rise to this realm."

He brought me to the goddess of the planet—a being of immense divine feminine light, stronger even than Gaia in resonance.

Her name: Lida.

She told me, "You are here to anchor the dimensions of this world into yourself and the client—and then into the Earth collective."

So, we did.

The energy was unlike anything I've ever felt.

Then I was taken to a celestial council. They presented a cosmic orb—a sphere filled with pure, love-based deities and star beings prepared to assist this new universe outside the matrix.

They asked us to embody these beings into our celestial field, preparing Earth's transition.

And then... came the part I resisted.

They showed me the #1 being of density—the one whose grip held the consciousness of humanity down.

They told me, "Place the light in him."

I resisted.

I didn't want to touch him.

But I obeyed, quickly and without hesitation.

Immediately, my focus shifted.

I watched as he dissolved into five fallen archangels.

Christ opened a portal to the Womb of Creation and took them in—for rehabilitation.

At that moment, the density grid began dissolving.

What Does This Mean for Us?

There is so much more happening behind the veil than most realize.

Channeling is not just speaking to a voice.

It is remembering our divine relationships—our missions forged in the light before form, in realms before realms.

Some of you reading this are meant to channel.

Some of you already are—but don't know the full story of who you're working with.

Let this transmission serve as a reminder:

You are ancient.

You are encoded.

And when the match is found, whole new realms open—not just to you, but through you, for all of Earth.

Now is the time.

Anchor the light.

And trust what is being born in you.

The Atlantean Lightbearer & the Mantis Treaty

A depiction of a 1-1 session

She was born into one of the wealthiest families in Atlantis—a lineage of privilege, power, and prominence. But even as a child, she turned her back on materialism and chose the path of divinity. Unlike her parents or siblings, she left home at an early age and found sanctuary by the sea, living among a small group of pure-hearted souls.

It was there, in harmony with the ocean, the sun, and the light, that her true self expanded into divine love. A living embodiment of purity and source connection.

Others took notice—some with pure intentions, others with shadowed ones.

One in particular approached her under the guise of collaboration. An elite figure, reminiscent of the power players we still see in today's world, convinced her to help identify and nurture the planet's most gifted children. The client, full of heart, agreed—and what unfolded was nothing short of miraculous. These children were activated in incredible ways.

But behind the scenes, a hidden agenda was at play.

This elite was in covert partnership with the Mantis beings, who were researching the link between divine light and DNA activation. Their race sought to become god-like creators but lacked the understanding that true divinity cannot be taken—it must be lived. The Mantis believed that by abducting these radiant children, they could connect to their light and evolve.

They missed the sacred truth:

Ascension is an inward journey, one of devotion and pure relationship with the light.

It cannot be borrowed. It cannot be stolen.

At this point in the session, I connected to Mother God, unsure how to proceed. She revealed that the Mantis race had eventually come to regret their actions. Their offspring carried deep karmic wounds from this manipulation, and the race signed a universal treaty not to repeat this error.

So, we began healing.

Through divine intervention, we helped the Mantis release the karma, and we returned all the light that had been taken from the children. We healed their wounds across timelines and restored their full soul power to where they exist now.

And then another layer revealed itself.

The client was also part of the Pleiadian Alliance during a pivotal moment in Earth's galactic history. A time when certain forces attempted to tilt Earth's axis to disrupt Gaia's divine orbital path—an act that would have severed many of the natural flows of love, light, and frequency.

Aligned with the Pleiadians, Lyrans, and Arcturians, the client worked through the crystalline network of Earth to restore Gaia's natural axis and anchor harmonic frequencies. That restoration is what allows us now, in this time, to receive pillar alignments, solar upgrades, and consciousness acceleration.

As this was revealed, the energy that came through was blinding—some of the highest light frequencies I have ever witnessed in session.

It confirmed something I have long known:

The work we do here—whether remembered or not—changes everything.

The ascension is real. The shift is happening. And it is being guided by those who remember.

To this client, and to all who walk the light path—thank you.

Together, we are shifting the planet.

You Cannot Vanquish the Dark Heart

A depiction of a 1-1 session

You cannot make war with the dark heart.

It will always lead to destruction.

It must be healed from within.

Sometimes, 1-on-1 sessions feel like a full cinematic film. This session was exactly that.

The client, a Sirian being, began with a memory: a high-level meeting with the Sirian Council. A new species had just achieved interplanetary status—the Reptilians—and began invading a planet to extract a rare resource that would expand their fleets and technology. Though primitive by galactic standards, their agenda was dangerous enough to warrant action.

The client was dispatched to investigate. Despite being billions of years ahead in technology, the Sirians refused to engage in war. Instead, they met with the planet's royal family to offer tactical support for planetary defense.

But something unexpected happened.

The Reptilians had secretly developed a galactic weapon, brought it through another dimension, and unleashed it without warning. In an instant—like a Death Star activation—the planet's defenses were obliterated. The Sirians intervened just in time to remove the weapon and evacuate the royal family to a starship, where they gathered with the Galactic Council.

A decision was made: attempt peace negotiations. They boarded the Reptilian ambassador's quarters during his sleep to discuss resolution, but it was clear—there would be no peace. The meeting ended, and the ambassador was returned to his domain.

Time passed. The Reptilians continued advancing—faster than anticipated. The Council foresaw an attack on a Pleiadian planet, an advanced world that resembled Atlantis. Precautionary meetings were held with the Pleiadians, and preparations were made.

Sure enough, thousands of years later, the Reptilians launched their offensive—and were swiftly destroyed. But they didn't give up. Instead, they began infiltration through trade.

They tricked a young man dating the Pleiadian princess into a bad deal, indebting him with his life. The princess, desperate to save him, boarded a Reptilian ship to negotiate without telling her father. When her father found out, he stormed in, only to discover the truth behind the manipulation. The Reptilians agreed to release both captives—but only if granted access to the Pleiadian Ring for trade.

This deception would spark one of the largest galactic wars ever known.

The Pleiadians lost most of their fleet. The Reptilians were nearly wiped out—reduced to a few hidden outposts.

But they waited. Thousands of years hiding, secretly building a new galactic fleet with stolen intelligence. And then, when the time was right, they returned—and annihilated the Pleiadian home world.

In the aftermath, the Sirians reconvened. They realized a devastating truth:

No matter how many times the dark heart is defeated, it will rise again.

You cannot vanquish it. You must heal it.

Thus, the Earth matrix plan was born: to trap the dark heart within a grid of healing, where it could be transformed from the inside.

This session was a profound reminder of why we're here—why this healing work matters. As we heal ourselves, we heal the collective—Reptilians included.

You are not ready for interstellar communion until you are at peace within.

The Father Appears in Atlantis

Another facet of the session

She sat on a hilltop in full Christ Consciousness, gazing at the city of Atlantis. That day, a new crystal technology was being activated in the tower.

Drawn by the energy, she walked to the tower and ascended to the lab via a magnetic-propelled glass elevator. The head engineers greeted her with curiosity and respect.

They showed her how the device could program higher frequencies—potentially allowing bio-location, access to higher dimensions, and the opening of human potential. She asked if she could gather a few high-frequency friends for an experiment.

Four divine beings entered the crystal chamber. As the frequency dial rose—they vanished.

In the cosmos, they awoke as celestial beings—and a fifth voice emerged. It was the voice of the Creator. The Creator revealed the origins of time, the truth of Oneness, and the presence of both the Mother and Father of all creations.

When the dial was turned back, they reappeared. But now, there were five.

Standing before them was a being with a lion's head, radiant gemstones on his chest, and robes of cosmic royalty.

He said:

"I am the Father.

You may improve this device to safely reach other timelines and dimensions.

It may also be used to attune collective fields—cities, populations, entire groups."

In that moment, the client used the technology to attune humanity to higher octaves of frequency.

The Father then vanished.

The engineers saw nothing—but those who had ascended saw it

all. Because only those vibrating at the frequency of creation could perceive him.

They brought the teachings back and continued refining the device to unlock its true divine potential.

The Rise of the Seraphim Angelic Incarnate Collective

A depiction of a 1-1 session

Above the client's energy field shimmered a heavenly radiance. As I followed the energy upward, we arrived in the Halls of Love within the heavenly realms—an exalted space of divine grace.

There, her Seraphim angelic self sat in luminous serenity, smiling ear to ear, writing in golden letters on a parchment woven from the frequencies of light. Each stroke of her pen, dipped in the ink of creation, danced with angelic light language—a sacred script carrying the blueprint of divine orchestration.

As I tuned into the deeper meaning of these radiant letters, a majestic vision unfolded:

A new creation was activating—the incarnation of Seraphim angels across all galactic systems, including Earth.

I saw Stargates encoded with Seraphim frequencies connecting realms, timelines, and planets. These portals of divine radiance were opening, allowing Seraphim codes to flow across the multiverse.

Her scroll, a divine instrument, began to heal the Seraphim heart, restoring the heavenly crown to each. And then, something profound occurred—

The scroll initiated the unification of all Seraphim hearts, linking them through time, space, and dimensional veils to form a collective Seraphim Heart Field.

This radiant network reached:

Incarnate Seraphim souls on Earth

Ethereal Seraphim in heavenly realms

Seraphim aspects within galactic civilizations

It raised the angelic fields, enhanced heart-based energetic architecture, and brought divine alignment to planetary systems.

The client—a Seraphim Commander of Divinity—was filled with joyful reverence. Her sacred scroll was now ready to fulfill its divine mission: to activate and bind the Seraphim Collective in heart, service, and radiance across all realities.

She waited lifetimes for this moment.

And now, it has begun.

So blessed we are to find one another again.

So blessed are the hearts of heaven, now awakened on Earth.

A 1-1 Depiction of a Heart Healing So Grand — From Our Beloved Stars

A depiction of a sacred session

Many are unaware there was once a time on Earth when the dark defeated the light, ruling in absolute distortion, wretched and cruel. The Divine, in infinite wisdom, allowed for a temporary reign of darkness, knowing that one day, a great cleansing of all density would come.

This was the Dark Age of mankind, where nearly all were possessed by the reflection of the dark heart, living as distorted versions of their divine selves.

But as that dark time neared its end, the stars themselves incarnated. Among them was the client—an embodiment of the North

Star—who stood in sacred ceremony with other incarnate star beings, fully in their God consciousness, preparing to heal the dark reflection and usher in the new age.

Now, once again, the time has come.

In this session, she returned to complete the ancient star ceremony, and it began with a force I had never felt so deeply before:

A universal love so powerful, it overwhelmed the field. Following up her pillar of light, I was met by Kali Ma, in her full universal power, enveloping the client in fierce divine love and protection—securing the sacred space so the ceremony could begin.

Within the ceremonial circle, star beings gathered again. It was agreed: Each star would hold a human heart in their hands.

At the center, the client—the North Star—radiated a divine command. Her light, bright and unwavering, began to amplify and spin, merging with all stars and transmitting the highest divine frequency into the hearts of all connected souls, healing them of the reflections of darkness.

Then, Christ entered the field, offering the keys to the Mother-Father Creator frequency—fusing the awakened hearts with their divine blueprints, so that each soul could now reflect the light within, and not the pain of the past.

This session was one for the ages—a cosmic turning point that signaled the dissolution of dark reflections within all beings.

It is truly an honor to be present in such a time, with such greatness, and to witness this sacred work unfold.

Infinite gratitude to the client,

to the stars,

to the angels,

and to the Divine orchestration that brought this healing into being.

The new age is here.

The Hidden Story of Agartha

A depiction of a 1-1 session

This was the first time I had ever seen an Agarthan Aspect come through in a session—and what unfolded was nothing short of extraordinary.

The Agarthans originate from another dimension—a peaceful, evolved galactic civilization known across universes for their role as peacemakers and universal helpers. Their home planet thrives in abundance and harmony, with advanced technologies powered by a blue crystalline mineral—an energetic resource integral to their fertility and life force.

In time, their native supply of this blue mineral began to deplete, and with it, their fertility rates declined. Facing the gradual decline of their species, they discovered that Earth held an abundance of this mineral, accessible through dimensional overlays. Thus began the Agarthan migration to Earth.

The Client's Role

The client, an explorer and high-ranking emissary of kindness from the Agarthan Council, was a pioneer of the Earth mission. She led the early migration teams and helped establish their first subterranean base—not in Antarctica initially, but in a crystalline, mineral-rich region farther east.

Using quantum technologies, the Agarthans could manipulate matter and energy to create instant structures. With only a few commands, vast crystalline temples and energy centers would materialize from thin air.

As time passed, the Agarthans noticed disturbing activity: deep core drilling into Gaia's crust, orchestrated by a faction that included Atlantean Pleiadians and Mantis beings. Alarmed, the Agarthans conducted a stealth investigation—disguising their arrival among a pod of whales in the sea above the drilling site.

What they discovered was deeply troubling. The beings on board discussed harnessing Earth's inner power—not to uplift humanity, but to weaponize it for planetary control. However, they were being influenced by another darker force, still unrevealed.

Strategic Defense & The Hidden Agenda

The client returned to Agartha and presented her findings. The Council determined that this operation posed an extinction-level threat to Earth. Although inherently nonviolent, the Agarthans made the decision to neutralize the military facility quietly and swiftly. The destruction was executed with minimal suffering, and healing was immediately sent to the souls who perished.

Though many Pleiadians were benevolent, a rogue faction in high command had secretly allied with the Mantis beings—who themselves had fallen under the corrupting influence of the Annunaki. These few acted out of greed and lust for control, endangering Earth's future.

A trusted Pleiadian general, having learned of the infiltration, sought out the Agarthans and confirmed the truth. He warned them of an impending attack and bought time for the client to relocate their most advanced technology—a device that could transform matter into any other form—to a new base in Antarctica, where the magnetic fields offered a strategic advantage.

The Arrival of the Annunaki & The Great Earth War

After the failed Pleiadian attack, the Annunaki arrived, revealing their true intent: to conquer Earth, destroy its races, and claim the planet for themselves. What followed was the greatest war Earth has ever known—the highest technologies of the Agarthans and their allies against the darkest powers of the Annunaki.

Massive destruction followed. But before the client perished, she rescued and protected a portion of humanity, fulfilling her original mission to safeguard Earth's evolution.

It was from this point that the Inner Earth Alliance was born—a sacred coalition of races who would protect Earth from within, as the surface of the planet endured manipulation and chaos. While the Annunaki were powerful enough to overtake most races, they were ultimately defeated, and the Councils of Nibiru lost all claim to Earth. The Annunaki were fully ejected from the planet many months ago.

The Activation of the Agarthan Blueprint

During this session, we reactivated the full Agarthan blueprint embedded in the genetic and energetic memory of galactic races and human incarnates who carry Agarthan lineage. This included the retrieval of advanced knowledge, healing technologies, and crystalline codes stored in Agarthan data systems.

As a result, many souls on Earth will now awaken to their Agarthan selves, the part of them that came to guide, heal, and uplift this planet from the inside out.

 This session is a cosmic milestone.

It reveals the deeper truth of why Inner Earth exists, and why so many feel called to protect, heal, and remember.

Agartha has returned. And with it,

the divine guardians of Earth.

The Sessions I Live For

A sacred depiction of two divine 1-on-1 sessions

The Supper of the Christed Heart

A soft pink light began emanating from the client, and I followed it upward—ascending through her field—until it reached her Uni Source, the level of her oversoul and divine origin.

There, I was greeted by the Goddess of Diamond Light. She looked upon me with radiant clarity and said,

"She must become one with Christ today."

Moments later, Christ appeared, and we were instantly transported into a divine supper—not the Last Supper, but a sacred celebration with his disciples gathered in joy. They laughed, drank wine, broke bread, and shared in the overflowing love of the Christed heart.

Then, I watched as each of them intentionally linked their heart energy together in a powerful pink current of unconditional love. It flowed like a rose river through every soul present.

Christ turned to us and said:

"This is how you must love others—as we are loving each other now, in unconditional love."

One of the disciples asked:

"How can we bring this love with us always? How can we remember this feeling?"

Christ responded:

"Cherish this as your most prized possession. Remember this as the love we have for one another. Let it be the way you treat all beings—as the Divine Being you are."

He continued:

"Do not be at quarrel. Others may be—but it is not for you to match that. How can you live as your divine self—and guide others to do the same—if you are in quarrel? Be peace. With yourself. With others.

Deceive me not. Bring your heart to me as it is. In truth. I will love it unconditionally. Only in this way—truth and honesty—will we heal the tribulations together."

Later in the session, a past timeline was revealed. Before the era of Christ, the client had played a messiah-type role in ancient Egypt, serving as a divine voice of wisdom for her people.

This was a powerful reminder that many are unaware of the sacredness they hold, and yet—they are profoundly pure and divinely encoded.

Diamond Activations & The Ascended Integration

In a second session that same day, a tremendous presence appeared and gently greeted me:

"Hi David. I'm Sophia."

The Diamond Mother herself had arrived to facilitate activations with the client.

Sophia guided me to an ascended version of the client and explained:

"She must now fully integrate with her ascended self."

I asked, "Is this who she becomes once she ascends?"

Sophia answered:

"No, this is her ascended self."

We began the merging. Her ascended self cleared layers of shadow reflections, dissolving what no longer served. Then, Sophia told me something unexpected:

"You must disconnect her from Gaia's portals—and the portals of this universe—and anchor her instead into her ascended light."

I hesitated. "Won't she disappear from this matrix reality if I do that?"

Sophia replied:

"How can one fully ascend if they still carry Gaia's portals within them?"

I turned to the client and said, "Let's do it. You'll be okay."

And so we began. I disconnected her from Gaia's internal portal grid, then from the universal constructs—and anchored her entirely into her divine, ascended self.

What happened next was beyond imagination.

We were lifted above the celestial dome, a luminous grid above the stars that stores every soul's ascension story. For the first time, I witnessed the entire light-being collective gathered there.

Side by side as our ascended aspects, the client and I placed a sacred crystal into Gaia's core, coded with divine blueprint instructions for all who are ready. As the crystal activated, Ascended Masters emerged from it—radiant and alive—flowing into the fields of those prepared to receive their guidance.

This moment felt like a marker of planetary preparation—a signal the critical mass point is near.

These activations plant the seed for the collective leap, for those who have long been walking the path of remembrance.

And to me,

this is what it's all about.

The Omega Activation and the Free Zone Realignment

Some sessions are so profound they echo across dimensions—and this was one of them.

As the higher self collective continues to merge into Earth, a new presence begins to rise within the client. I feel it, brilliant and expansive.

Suddenly, the Omega Aspect of the client comes forward.

Omega—the level just beneath Prime Source itself—holds a purity so divine, it can only be accessed by those embodying the uppermost layers of consciousness.

As she merges with this Omega self, a doorway of light opens— not metaphorically, but quite literally in the quantum. We are pulled through it and arrive at a pivotal point in Earth's hidden history:

The formation of the Inner Earth Kingdoms.

The Rise of the Free Zone

The client is instantly referred to as a Star Mother—a high-frequency Pleiadian ET who was part of the sacred alliance to birth Lemuria, Telos, and Agartha. These three inner sanctums, though independently formed, were designed in harmony as a triangular energetic network deep beneath the Earth.

Together, they formed what was called:

The Free Zone

A holy domain where war could never occur, and purity was preserved beyond the interference of dark agendas.

The crystalline pyramids of these three city hubs each held a power source—a diamond core resembling a Vogel crystal on divine overdrive. These crystalline cores, once synchronized, generated a planetary frequency of purity so high that:

No lower-dimensional beings could enter,

No interdimensional portals could be accessed,

And the cross-field grid of interdimensional travel was sealed within the Free Zone.

The Second-Tier Activation

Due to her direct involvement in the formation of this sacred domain, the client was able to unlock the second tier of this crystalline network—a frequency transmission system that resonates throughout Earth and all dimensions tethered to this reality.

As the frequencies expanded outward in harmonic waves, something unprecedented occurred...

The Liberation of the Deities

Two of the great cosmic Deities—Kali Ma and Shiva—who have for eons held both the templates of light and dark within them for cosmic balance, stepped forward.

In response to the purity of the Free Zone reactivation,

they willingly released their dark templates—not into chaos, but into sacred recycling tubes generated by this planetary shift. These tubes are designed to transmute density into crystalline light.

It was a cosmic offering of completion. A moment where even the most integrated polarities were ready to transcend darkness as a necessity.

At that moment, Earth changed.

As above, so below.

As within, so without.

The Beginning of Purity-Based Reality

This session marks the turning point of humanity's energetic timeline:

The end of dark constructs as foundational elements.

A return to purity—not as an escape from duality, but as the natural evolution beyond it.

The Free Zone lives again, not just as a place in Inner Earth, but now as a broadcast field of harmony and crystalline remembrance available to all who tune to it.

Final Words

To the Earth Ambassadors, the Star Mothers, and the Deities of Love who show up in these sessions:

Your presence is rewriting Earth's story.

You are not remembering history—you are completing it.

It is an eternal honor to witness these transmissions unfold.

My First Life: The Genesis of Galactic Mastery

A Journey into the Origin of My Soul's Evolution

Recently, I had the profound and humbling experience of returning to my first life—the inception point of my soul's journey.

What I witnessed was not primitive, nor infantile—but magnificently advanced, beyond anything Earth has imagined.

The Planet of Origins

I found myself on a futuristic, interstellar planet, architecturally radiant and alive with consciousness.

The city stretched across land and sea, seamlessly interconnected by elegant, bridge-like highways that moved not just physical bodies—but frequency, intention, and freedom.

The buildings rose like temples of light—cathedral-style structures with circular domes, triangular facades, and flowing geometries.

Their surfaces shimmered with hues of golden bronze, teal, light grey, and crystalline white—each color embedded with energetic significance.

It wasn't just beautiful, it was harmonic. The entire city was a living expression of collective mastery.

Training in the Disciplines of Expression

From birth, we are immersed in a curriculum rooted in conscious expression mastery.

Every thought, gesture, and intention is a chance to refine awareness and master that field of being.

Each discipline of life—from joy to sorrow, from presence to creation—is symbolized by a unique sigil. These aren't just teachings. They are living frequencies we attune to, and by doing so, we earn mastery over aspects of self and life.

This system instilled in us a foundation:

"All expressions are sacred. All awareness is a gateway. All mastery begins within."

Galactic Contribution and Soul Reputation

Upon completion of mastery on my home planet, I stepped into my galactic role.

As an emissary of consciousness, I met and formed alliances with beings from countless civilizations.

Because I fully embodied the disciplines of expression, I was seen as wise, grounded, and profoundly relatable. This made it easy to forge interstellar bonds and contribute meaningfully to councils and civilizations.

The Thesis That Changed Everything

I initiated my galactic thesis on an uncharted field of consciousness:

Bio-relocation through self-projection and space-bending.

At the time, no one had achieved this form of teleportation through pure consciousness. But this research gained traction and soon became a full planetary curriculum, birthing an entire consciousness university system. This marked the beginning of what would later be called the Framework of Light Expansion—a universal blueprint still used by many.

Gene Printing & The Sharing of Gifts

In a sacred alliance of advanced beings, we created a planet of higher training where all were invited to share their gifts.

We developed a revolutionary process: Gene Printing of Gifts— where beings could download, encode, and embed their spiritual gifts into their genetic signature, making them permanent within their lineage.

This wasn't imitation—it was sacred collaboration.

We weren't hoarding abilities. We were weaving divinity into biology.

The Secret to Rapid Evolution: Anchoring into Consciousness Itself

One of the most transformative revelations came through this truth:

Every study has a consciousness.

To master a subject, anchor into the highest version of its

consciousness.

If we studied telekinesis, we didn't study from theory—we connected directly with the consciousness of telekinesis, already perfect and embodied. This allowed immediate, quantum-level acceleration of abilities.

Imagine if Earth did this now.

Imagine every student anchoring into the pure frequency of their chosen path, from art to architecture, from healing to innovation.

We would evolve in decades what would otherwise take millennia.

Why I Returned

I chose to return and reawaken my first life's mastery to activate the domino effect.

From this life onward, I saw timeline after timeline—consciousness schools, planetary councils, and breakthroughs in universal wisdom.

This is why I teach.

This is why I serve.

This is why I remember.

To carry forth the Legacy of the First Light. Not to dominate, but to liberate potential, together as a collective soul species.

In Closing

We were never meant to journey alone.

We came to activate each other, share gifts, expand light, and return to truth as one.

As we rise, we do not rise as isolated stars,

but as a constellation of mastery,

guiding the way for all who are ready to remember.

With deepest love and remembrance,

The Sound of Love

Working with the Fae Realm for Divine Union

A 1-on-1 Session Account on How the Fairies Assist Humanity in Love's Grandest Calling

In this session, we entered a realm where few have tread consciously—

The Fae Realm, keepers of joy, magic, and divine love union.

My client had long dreamt of her divine partner, a soul she had not yet met in the physical, but who appeared in visions and dreams for many years.

I had once been shown by the Fae that fairies assist in divine partnerships, guiding the meeting of destined lovers through unseen threads of frequency.

So I knew exactly where to go.

The Song of Love

Upon entering the client's field and calling forth her fairy guide, we were immediately greeted with joy. The fairy, shimmering in a soft iridescent glow, said the first step was to connect to the "song of love."

"Every soul has a song," she told us.

"Your client has a song, and so does her beloved. And when those songs harmonize, it creates a frequency bridge, this is how we connect them."

The expression "love is in the air" suddenly made perfect sense—it refers to these sacred songs, floating in the ether, waiting to harmonize and call one another home.

As we attuned to the client's song of love, the fairies brought us to ancient tree portals—living sentinels of union energy.

With the guidance of her fae companion, we sent her soul's song across the tree grid to reach her divine partner, activating a magnetic pull.

The Celebration Before the Meeting

The fairies then pulled back the veil to reveal something extraordinary:

A full celebration of her divine union had already begun in the fae realm.

There were songs, flutes, drums, and laughter.

Fairies danced in rings of joy, playing the melody of the union to come.

They celebrate before the physical meeting because, to the fae, the union already exists.

Time to the Fae is a living rhythm—not a line—and they honor divine timing by singing it into being.

The Divine Instruction

Then came a regal moment—

The Mother of Fairies herself arrived, radiating golden-pink starlight.

She said:

"Let's co-create the divine instruction. It is time for this sacred meeting to occur."

With a quill of light, she inscribed on a golden scroll of fairy light language—a set of codes and instructions for all fairies across the realms.

This scroll was then delivered to the trees so that every fairy guardian of union energy could begin weaving the sequence of synchronicities necessary for the meeting to unfold.

The Perfect Moment

Fairies don't just align one event—they align all events. They began constructing what they called the Perfect Moment Energy—a weave of small decisions, chance encounters, timing, courage, and heart openings leading to the destined meeting.

"Each right moment leading up to the meeting," they said,

"is a note in the love song we are singing."

So they sing each step forward. Each step is a victory. Each moment is sacred.

The Union Code Keepers

At the end of the session, the fairies revealed their most sacred guardians:

The Union Code Keepers.

These are specialized fairies who hold the divine union blueprint for each soul and their partner.

Each keeper holds the encoded frequency of love that magnetizes the pair—a unique vibration that cannot be replicated.

They said:

"To bring forth union in physical, one must work with their union code keepers.

These codes are dormant in both until they are activated.

When activated, they begin pulling the souls together through resonance, not logic."

We were guided to activate the client's divine love union codes and instructed to tune in regularly, feeling them merge and harmonize—just like the two songs becoming one.

In Closing

This session wasn't just a glimpse into divine union—it was a living transmission of how the fairy realms support human love.

They are the whisperers of synchronicity, the architects of the meeting, the singers of sacred love songs.

To all divine lovers seeking union:

Your songs are being sung.

Your codes are being activated.

The fairies are at work.

Allow the magic to unfold.

Allow the perfect moment to arrive.

It's already written in the scrolls of love.

A Heart for Every Trouble

Inspired by a 1-on-1 Session with Angelic Realms and Timeless Healing

From the realms above, a message of healing arrived.

The client and I were guided into a vision that the angels asked to be shared with everyone—a simple yet profound healing practice that anyone can use at any time:

Visualize your angelic teams above you.

See them sending down heart-shaped pulses of pure love.

Each heart enters your body, finding one of your troubles.

As the heart vibrates, it completely transmutes the trouble with divine love.

Trouble by trouble, heart by heart, you are healed.

Repeat this visualization until you feel lighter, clearer, and freer. This is not just a meditation—it is a soul recalibration.

The angels say, "There is a heart for every trouble. Always."

The Modality of Mary of Cleophas

A 1-on-1 Session Unlocks Ancient Physical Healing Wisdom

The client, a star soul of divine remembrance, came into session holding within her the codes of one of the most powerful yet little-known healers in biblical history:

Mary of Cleophas, sister of Mother Mary.

As soon as we entered her field the teams of light brought us back in time to a moment where divine healing was needed for one of the brothers of Christ.

He sustained a deep wound on his right calf, speared by a Roman soldier, and infection had begun to set in.

Then, Mary of Cleophas approached him with divine calm.

She revealed a modality of miraculous healing—now remembered in this session.

The Alpha Omega Light Sphere

Mary placed her hands together and generated a radiant sphere of Alpha Omega light.

This light was the original blueprint light of creation and completion, sourced beyond time.

She placed the orb into the center of his brain, and it illuminated every brain cell.

The nervous system lit up like constellations in the sky.

Calling the Elohim

Next, she invoked the Elohim angels, masters of divine architecture and healing rays.

Their light poured into the body, expanding the capacity of the healing field.

Then she did something extraordinary—

She blended her divine frequency with theirs, creating a combined stream of multi-dimensional healing light.

She flowed this light from the brain down the body, anchoring healing at every level.

The Secret: Divine Instructions

Here was the most important step—and the "secret sauce," as the angels called it:

Mary didn't simply intend healing.

She gave divine instructions.

She spoke directly to the subconscious mind, delivering specific divine instructions to restore health, clear infection, and regenerate tissue.

She encoded these instructions deep into the brain-mind-body connection, activating the body's divine template of healing.

This is the key difference between intentions and instructions:

Intentions are wishes.

Instructions are commands written in divine light.

Final Light Sealing

To conclude, Mary called once again on the Alpha Omega light and poured it throughout the wounds, covering the body like a shimmering force field.

It wasn't just healing—it was renewal.

This sacred process, revealed through this client, is now available for all who resonate.

The Healing Modality of Mary of Cleophas: A Step-by-Step

Alpha Omega Orb Creation

» Visualize a divine orb of Alpha Omega light between your hands.

» Place it in the center of your brain. Let it awaken your entire nervous system.

Call the Elohim

» Ask the Elohim to send their healing rays into your body.

» Blend their light with your divine frequency.

Stream Light Through the Body

» Flow this combined divine light from the brain down the body, infusing every cell and organ.

Give Divine Instructions

» Speak clearly and lovingly to your body.

» Example: "Regenerate this tissue. Clear this infection. Balance all systems. Return to divine wholeness."

Seal with Alpha Omega Light

» Flow the light over the wounds and body as a glowing shield of wholeness.

Final Note from the Angels:

"Your body remembers what your mind has forgotten. Speak to it as divine.

Give it the instructions it needs to return to love."

May all who read this remember the ancient ways of divine healing, and the truth that the greatest healers are simply those who remember the original blueprint of light.

When Gaia Volunteered for Earth

A Sacred Account of a 1-on-1 Session

The session begins as Christ enters and brings us to the angels.

From there, he takes us to a sacred lifetime of the client—back to when Earth was being formed.

The client, a part of a galactic evolutionary team, traveled between Gaia and her mothership, where councils held plans for the evolution of life across eternity. These councils discussed what elements needed to be placed where, what forms of life would emerge during specific periods of time, and how geography must support those evolutionary stages.

Another council meeting was called to discuss the source of Earth—a powerful core of divine energy that, in time, would attract beings seeking to harness it. It was clear: Earth needed a guardian, a protector of the source.

A council was formed with the presence of divine source, and galactic beings gathered to deliberate. Then, in a moment of unspeakable beauty, within a diamond-white brilliance, the Goddess Gaia appeared in her full divine form and declared:

"I volunteer."

The light from her heart was radiant beyond description.

Christ allowed me to follow her light backward—to learn where Gaia came from.

The Origin of Gaia

Gaia came from a magical training planet, filled with universal beings.

Some looked human but were made of sunlight.

Others, human in form, were made of starlight.

Gaia herself: a being of diamond-water light.

This planet was extraordinary.

There were both light beings and physical beings, all taking guidance from the universal ones—a group of eternal custodians holding the star consciousness, sun consciousness, and planetary evolution in their care.

They also guarded the divine records for all life.

Before Gaia volunteered, she formed her team. Among them was Melchizedek, appearing in his luminary form—working on establishing the divine order for Earth. He and others prepared the guardians and structures of light that would oversee Earth through every cycle, age, and transformation.

The Moment of Volunteering

Gaia entered the ship in full presence, and in front of all the divine beings, she offered to:

To bind herself to the Source of Earth.

To be its protector.

To be its guardian.

To serve the magical life that would one day emerge and evolve.

This session was a soul-level remembrance of that moment.

One of the most magical, reverent, and luminous sessions I have ever experienced.

The love that Gaia holds, the sacrifice, the guardianship, and the eternal vow—is why we walk this Earth at all.

"She didn't just become the Earth. She became the Source within it."

Attracting Divine Love

A True Depiction of a 1-1 Session

A client has graciously agreed to share the powerful journey of their healing, as divinely guided through a private 1-on-1 session. This account reveals how deep wounds—emotional, karmic, and ancestral—were lovingly cleared to attract a divine love partner.

What follows is a detailed overview of how the relationship healing was performed, the spiritual structures supporting it, and why this work is so essential on the path to sacred partnership.

The Healing Process

Setting the Sacred Space and Angelic Assistance

Sacred Space: A field of divine protection is created, calling upon the Archangels to surround and hold the session in higher light.

Higher Self and Angelic Teams: The client's higher self and angelic guides are called in to oversee the healing that occurs, offering precise light-coded guidance and divine support throughout.

Heart Wound Clearing & Frequency Alignment Multidimensional Heart Wounds: The client's heart field reveals pain from past lifetimes. These frequencies are held gently, brought into awareness, and transmuted.

Frequency Alignment: By healing these wounds, the client's energy field begins to vibrate in divine resonance, magnetizing a partner who matches this upgraded frequency.

Akashic Records and Root Trauma Retrieval

Akashic Access: The record keepers are called in to reveal root traumas buried in soul memory.

Root Healing: These origin wounds—often the blueprint behind recurring relationship pain—are cleared with divine love, restoring the soul's wholeness across time.

Core Relationship Wounds Transformed

Jealousy and Abuse

Jealousy: Often arising from emotional and physical wounds, jealousy is acknowledged and transmuted.

Abuse Healing: Trauma from emotional, physical, and sexual abuse is compassionately cleared. Soul fragments are retrieved and reintegrated into the light body.

Cheating and Betrayal

Infidelity Wounds: Past-life and current-life cheating is brought forward. The client forgives themselves and others, healing the root of mistrust.

Betrayal: Pain around betrayal is connected to self-worth and dissolved through unconditional love.

Insecurity and Dishonesty

Insecurity: Emotional wounds stemming from unavailable or dishonest partners are gently healed.

Dishonesty Patterns: All echoes of deceit are released from the client's field, clearing pathways for honest, secure connection.

Codependency and Trust Issues

Codependency: Mistrust and unworthiness loops are severed, freeing the client from energetic entanglement.

Trust Restoration: Timelines and dimensions are cleared to rebuild authentic trust in self and future relationships.

Superiority Complex and Narcissism

Power Imbalances: Past entanglements with narcissistic or dominant partners are released.

Self-Awareness: Any reflected narcissistic patterns within are acknowledged, healed, and brought back into divine balance.

Shock and Emotional Shutdown

Shock Release: Shock fields from past abuse that caused emotional shutdown are cleared from the nervous system.

Emotional Reawakening: The client's heart is lovingly restored to openness and peace.

The Sacred Heart Awakening

With the clearing complete, the Sacred Heart is awakened. This multi-dimensional frequency expansion allows the client to become the divine partner they wish to attract.

Higher Heart Expansion: The client radiates compassion, unconditional love, and inner unity.

Frequency of Divine Union: The timeline is opened for a partner to meet them in this same frequency of healed, whole love.

Angelic Assistance in Partner Alignment

Guardian Angels: The client's guardian angels work behind the scenes to weave the perfect meeting moment.

Divine Timeline Activation: New timelines are opened for sacred union—ones built on purity, loyalty, and emotional presence.

Why This Healing Matters

This is not just relationship healing. This is soul evolution, timeline clearing, and frequency re-coding.

Holistic Transformation: Emotional, physical, and spiritual wounds are addressed simultaneously across all dimensions.

Everything is Connected: Healing one pattern (e.g., jealousy) often releases many patterns (e.g., codependency, mistrust).

Self-Forgiveness is Key: The act of forgiving oneself is the gateway to divine love.

Frequency is Everything: When your heart, soul, and frequency align with divine love, you become a mirror of it.

Empowered Conscious Creation: You become aware of your patterns, rewrite them, and consciously attract a new experience of love.

Final Reflection

True relationship healing is deep soul art.

By committing to this level of work, you clear lifetimes of pain, retrieve your soul's truth, and prepare to meet your match in divine love—not from longing or lack, but from embodied wholeness.

This sacred session was one of many now occurring across the planet as humanity enters into its divine partnership era.

It is time. Love is returning.

Falling From Grace

A Sacred Account from a 1-1 Session

In a recent session, a client asked a powerful question:

"Why do my guides keep saying I was chosen?"

What followed was a stunning remembrance—a divine transmission revealing one of the greatest stories hidden in the angelic records: the true meaning of "falling from grace."

The Angel of Grace and the Great Fall

Long ago, in the angelic realms before the fall, the client's best friend was the Angel of Grace—an ethereal being who embodied divine harmony, reverence, and heart-aligned elegance.

During the great fall, as chaos rippled through the angelic kingdoms, the dark forces captured Grace herself. She was forcefully pulled out of Heaven and brought into the dense realms of physical incarnation. As above, so below—when Grace fell, grace left the collective consciousness of humanity.

This was the moment when morality fractured. Without grace, humanity slowly lost its ethical compass. Immorality, cruelty, and emotional disconnection became possible on Earth. The term "falling from grace" was not just symbolic—it was literal. The Angel of Grace had fallen.

The Mission to Bring Grace Back

In the higher councils, the client and the angelic orders devised a plan: they would bring Grace back.

But the challenge was immense. Each time Grace incarnated on Earth, the fallen ones would give her great riches, status, and power—not as a blessing, but as a distraction. These gifts were designed to sever her connection from her angelic self, to make her forget the love and humility of Heaven.

Despite the angelic guides working tirelessly from above, Grace could not remember.

So, the angels made a bold decision: they chose to incarnate, too. To walk among humanity and teach grace again—not just to Grace, but to all.

This is why the client was chosen.

She didn't fall—she volunteered. She came to Earth to restore Grace to her rightful place in the collective heart of humanity.

The Breakthrough in Session

In the session, the location of Grace's current incarnation on Earth was discovered. With the help of the angelic teams, we were able to clear Grace's field, reconnect her angelic heart, and restore her consciousness to its divine light template.

At that moment, the client formed a new bond—an angelic heart fusion with Grace herself.

Grace, once lost, was welcomed back into the heavenly energies.

The Gift of Healing Separation

Now, with this restored connection, the client holds the divine codes to heal separation consciousness.

In her presence, others feel more connected to their divine essence. Through her sessions, people experience:

A return to unity

The dissolving of inner division

The awakening of self-love through divine grace

The client is now a living embodiment of grace consciousness. Those who receive healing through her connection to the Angel of Grace will find themselves more anchored in their truth, more centered in love, and more aligned with the divine.

Final Reflection

This sacred session was not just a personal healing—it was a collective restoration.

Grace has returned.

And through the client, she now walks among us again—softly, lovingly, and powerfully.

There will always be a place in my heart for the Angel of Grace, and for those who choose to help humanity remember her.

The Lost Light of Mars

A 1-1 Session Revelation: The Diamond Mothers and the Return of Mars' Golden Grid

I always knew there was a good side to Mars before the takeover... but, for the first time, it was revealed in this session. And wow—how amazing to rediscover this gem from the past.

Something truly extraordinary unfolded. The client had just returned from a journey to Ireland, and when I connected with her higher self, I saw she was holding a massive ball of light. She said,

"I've gathered all this energy. Can you help me unpack them?"

As I peered into the sphere, I saw rows of white-light guardians—beings of the highest frequency—lining up in front of a Stargate portal. This was a gateway to one of the client's past lives.

I walked through.

What I saw stunned me.

The Forgotten Golden Mars

Mars—a flourishing planet of light.

Crystalline cities stretched across the horizon. The frequency was high, celestial. Ships soared through the sky. Humans—yes, humans—walked peacefully, serving as ambassadors of light. The land had green grass, flowing water streams, high technology, and radiant harmony.

There was even a familiar presence—a lady I had long seen in Lemuria, known as the Mother of the Lands. And here she was... on Mars.

The client had been a seer stationed at a galactic post on Mars. She worked directly with universal consulates from all corners of creation. An appointed mage in a communications center, she didn't need the advanced tech—she used it more for convenience. Others relied on it. But, she was it.

The Separation of Source

At this time, the separation from Source had recently occurred. All of Mars felt it. For the first time, emotional energies resembling depression and lower thought forms started to stir.

The Mars Embassy began broadcasting emotional updates to help the population adjust. They encouraged people to use frequency-enhancing technologies to balance their energy bodies and explained how to work through emotional discomfort.

But the client was already far beyond.

She had held this post for thousands of years.

Then came the moment she merged with a light being, receiving a powerful download.

The message was clear:

Mars would be taken over. A fall was coming.

And she was to lead the evacuation—methodically, in divine order.

Preserving the Diamond Mothers

The first to be protected were the purest of Mars—a group of women known as the Diamond Mothers.

These were human-like beings filled with pure love, always seeking to uplift others. They dedicated their lives to interstellar joy missions, creating opportunities for different species to unite through love and harmony.

They delighted in surprising each other with notes, giving gifts, telling jokes, and making life better for all.

They were the most heart-centered beings of the time.

Their hearts were too pure to remain for what was coming.

They were the first to be brought to Earth.

Earth: The Frontier of Light

Next came the higher octave beings—connected to intergalactic fleets—who evacuated and left the universe altogether.

But the most amazing realization:

Many beings from different galaxies and systems were intentionally choosing to go to Earth.

Earth was designated as the Frontier of Light—the place where all that was pure would stand firm, anchoring the frequencies of love during the coming era of darkness.

Even more fascinating, some souls ascended on Earth before the density arrived. These advanced ones became the key holders—guardians of the higher dimensions—who stayed above to hold the light for those below. They are still with us today.

They are sending their light codes now to all who are ready.

Reawakening the Mars Grid

As the session ended, the client was shown a high-frequency technology that she embedded long ago into the core of Mars.

Now was the time to activate it.

And as she did, I witnessed a breathtaking scene:

A massive transmutation occurred.

The dark grids and containment fields surrounding Mars began to dissolve.

The density evaporated... replaced by a golden radiance.

The higher grids of Mars reawakened.

A Message to the Frontiers of Light

This transmission is not just a memory.

It's an activation.

As you read these words, know this:

Special keys from the higher realms are coming through.

They are meant for the frontiers of light who are on Earth right now.

Those who came to hold the light through it all.

Those remembering who they are.

And so it begins.

The Return of the Luminaries: A 1-on-1 Session That Changed Everything

This session was on another level.

It not only answered questions I hadn't cracked yet, it connected long-missing dots between the Order of Melchizedek, Archangel Metatron, and a powerful presence I hadn't understood fully until now: the Luminaries.

This section is part session, part backstory—offering insight that may activate a deep knowing in many of you reading.

The Question That Opened the Portal

It started when the client asked,

"Can I ask a question for the theme of our session?"

Of course, I said yes.

She replied,

"Archangel Metatron keeps coming up for me. And so does Melchizedek. But I don't know why. Can you find out my connection?"

This immediately stirred something in me. I've been connected to Melchizedek for years—his Blue Flames of Ascension have guided many of my teachings. And Metatron was the first being I ever channeled. There was something significant about this.

The Energetic Interference

As soon as we began, a dark energy entered the field. A heavy, disruptive force.

I recognized the stench.

It was Archonic.

I immediately called in Christ, the Ascended Masters, and Archangel Michael to clear the interference. And they did. But I refused to continue until I was sure—completely sure—that all densities were removed across all spectrums of existence.

Then I asked Christ,

"What was that about?"

He said:

"They don't want you bringing these frequencies through. But continue—you are protected."

The Stargate of the Crystal Lotus

Suddenly, we were inside a past life where the client—revealed as Pleiadian royalty, possibly a queen—was bringing forward a massive crystalline technology.

It looked like a lotus-shaped crystalline stargate, and as it opened, a burst of white light poured out.

I froze.

I knew this light. Its frequency. I'd only seen it three times before in my life:

At the Petroforms in Manitoba, where the Great White Light Spirit appeared to me as a portal, and light beings came to work with the Indigenous long ago.

Behind the I AM house at Mount Shasta, where the sacred water spirit revealed itself as the Great White Light.

And the very next day, when three Lemurian light beings emerged and showed me how to activate the Lemurian Heart.

Here it was again—but coming from technology?

How could that be?

The Luminaries Revealed

As I channeled Divine Mother, she told me:

"Go into the light."

I entered the frequency and saw the client's Pleiadian aspect, surrounded by beings of many star races. As the crystalline technology ignited, I saw Adama and other ascended masters fly out of the portal.

This was a Light Transporter.

The client had brought The Luminaries to Earth.

What happened next was stunning.

These radiant beings immediately manifested enchanted kingdoms, elemental realms, and realities beyond comprehension. Their manifesting abilities were so pure they began creating magic instantaneously and anchoring divine templates into Earth.

Enter Melchizedek

Then Melchizedek emerged from the portal.

I had to stop.

What was he doing here?

I went back to the Divine Mother for answers.

She said:

"Melchizedek is a Luminary, David. He's a Light Being. Do you remember in the Master Series when he took you to the Messiah Constellation and into the Cities of Light?"

"Yes," I answered.

"Those cities are the realms of the Luminaries. Melchizedek works across universes. He has been assisting Earth from the beginning of time. He is eternal, and this mission is galactic."

The Melchizedek Order and the Venusian-Lemurian Alliance

Suddenly it all clicked.

The Melchizedek Order, the Venusians, and the Lemurians have all been working together since Earth's inception. The Luminaries aren't just myth—they are the very Great Spirit behind the veil. The ones that countless spiritual traditions have spoken of, including Indigenous nations.

Look it up.

Search "Great Spirit", and you'll find:

"The Great Spirit is the supreme being and principal deity of Native American Indians. The Eye of Providence—God watching over humanity."

That eye—the Great Spirit—is not a singular deity.

It is a collective field of the Luminaries.

The light beings, the guardians, the watchers.

They are real. And they are here.

The Final Message from Metatron

At the end of the session, I channeled Archangel Metatron.

I asked,

"Why didn't the dark forces want this session to happen?"

His answer was thrilling:

"David, these frequencies remove the webs of deceit from Earth. The energies of deception are being dissolved. Soon, humans won't be able to lie anymore. It will be like the movie Liar Liar—truth will be vibrationally enforced. This is exciting!"

I felt the excitement.

I could feel it ripple through my entire being.

This wasn't just another session.

This was a reveal.

And now, the frequencies of the Luminaries are here for all of you.

The truth is returning.

Crystalline Codes, Mermaid Guardians & The Lotus Order: A 1-on-1 Session

Today's 1-1 session with the client was beyond extraordinary. She could have easily conducted the session herself, given how ready she is to distribute crystalline codes into the planetary field. What unfolded was nothing short of multidimensional brilliance and cosmic confirmation.

Andromedan Origins & Emotional Alchemy

We first connected to the client's Andromedan aspect—a radiant being of light who holds an advanced emotional recalibration modality similar to the Emotion Code. This healing system works by gently shifting out low emotional frequencies and lifting the vibratory rate of the client into alignment with crystalline wholeness.

The session immediately began raising the energy field, and we knew something sacred was unlocking.

The Crystal Fairy Realm Activation

Her higher self-opened a glowing dimensional doorway—revealing the Crystal Fairy Realm.

The client's crystal fairy aspect stepped forward, gracefully attuning her DNA to prepare for crystalline anchoring. Suddenly, crystal fairies began pouring through the veil, entering our reality and flying directly into our energetic grids.

It was enchanting—and deeply activating.

The Queen Mother Mermaid & The Purple Heart of Creation

That opening shifted everything.

A Queen Mother Mermaid emerged—an ancient aspect of the client—guarding what she called The Purple Heart of Creation, nestled deep in the ocean's sacred realms. It was held behind a protection field, untouched by interference, where mermaids in stasis awaited the signal to awaken.

Today was that day.

The mermaids are waking.

From the Purple Heart, a beam of source light erupted, shattering matrix overlays, opening the Ascension Gate, and reconnecting us to the Lemurian Lotus Order of Light—a realm of divine feminine mastery and ascended sacred knowledge.

The Lotus Heart Activation & High Priestess Light

The Ancient Ones of the Lemurian Lotus Order gathered and activated the Lotus of Light in the client's heart chakra—unfolding her into her High Priestess Light.

It was one of the most beautiful activations I've witnessed.

The inner earth Lemurians watched in awe.

I asked them, "Why didn't you open this gate yourselves?"

They replied:

"It had to be opened by humanity—to prove humanity is ready for ascension. It is sacred."

A Healer of the New Earth

The client is one of the most profound healers I've had the honor to work with.

What she activated today was not just a gift for herself—but for all of us. She is here to assist humanity in reconnecting to the divine templates of unity, grace, crystalline healing, and angelic love.

She will be one of the most desired healers of this era. Guaranteed.

Futuristic Earth, Pleiadian Technology & Christed Upgrades

Later that same day, another aspect of the client emerged—a Pleiadian frequency engineer from an Earth Origins Timeline—a time of pre-Lemurian crystalline peace, where the matrix didn't yet exist.

She showed me an Earth of towering crystal cities, stretching high into the sky and deep into the oceans. Shape-shifting was natural, mermaid-being forms were chosen freely, and nature thrived alongside technology.

This version of Gaia was breathtaking—and familiar.

It's the one we are ascending to.

The client's role?

She was operating a dimensional frequency development ship unlike any I've seen. Her ship could program and transmit dimensional upgrades—essentially designing the vibrational scaffolding for Earth's golden age.

Cosmic Cleansing & Timeline Boosts

From that ship, she projected a pure cleansing light, removing dark impressions from across the cosmos—planets, dimensions, and timelines.

Then came the Christ Magdalene Grail Line frequency.

A sacred upgrade activated across our current timeline—giving our Earth a beautiful vibrational boost. It was like watching the past reach into the present to heal and elevate the future.

The Universe is on Our Side

This session was a radiant reminder that:

The past is supporting the future.

Ancient aspects are uniting with the now.

Cosmic forces are upgrading humanity and the universal structure— through each client, session, and lightworker.

We are in the Golden Era of return.

Sessions like this are not just personal—they're planetary.

Yeshua's Pre-Human Mission & The Atlantean Heart Ascension

During this 1-on-1 session, we were blessed to witness something profoundly sacred.

The client expressed a close connection to Yeshua. What unfolded next was unexpected and breathtaking—we were shown a prehuman lifetime of Yeshua during the age of Atlantis.

Even then... he was preparing the way.

A Holy Order Beyond Earth

Yeshua, the client, and one other formed a holy triad—a sacred group of highest light initiates, likely Venusian in origin. Their mission was to prepare the portals of Earth for future ascension.

They walked to each of Earth's sacred centers, placing their light codes within them—not just for that time, but to seed Gaia with templates that would activate in the coming ascension age.

Their light became the foundation for higher dimensional ascension constructs.

Guardians of Encouragement

Beyond their sacred portal work, this triad also served as uplifters of spirit.

They often supported Pleiadian and galactic brothers and sisters who felt weary from being far from home and who began losing hope.

Through loving words, laughter, and divine reminder, they reignited their flame.

They spoke of the honor of serving the light and how every act of service mattered.

Their presence was unifying.

They lifted morale. They rekindled purpose. They healed fatigue with remembrance.

The Heart Ascension Activation Their uniting mission ignited multiple portals they had activated in the Atlantean era—portals that still exist today.

What they created sent a wave of heart ascension through Gaia:

It flowed into Gaia's core.

Rose back up through the Sphinx in Egypt—one of the ancient gateways.

And radiated out to the Celestial realms.

This frequency is now activating again.

As a result, a heart upgrade is arriving for all beings on Earth—softening density, awakening truth, and aligning the planet to the path of unity.

This session was more than remembrance.

It was confirmation that Yeshua's mission began far before his human embodiment.

This client played a pivotal role—then and now.

We are walking along the very path they prepared.

The portals are opening once more.

The Greatest War Timeline I've Ever Healed on Gaia

During this 1-on-1 session, I was brought into the most intense war timeline I've ever had the honor to clear on Earth.

The session began with a haunting king spirit energetically attached to the client—woven like a thick web across her consciousness. As I tuned deeper, the truth emerged:

The client was the sister of Cleopatra of Macedonia, directly connected to Alexander the Great, one of the most renowned conquerors in history.

The Restless Spirit of Alexander

Shockingly, Alexander's spirit was still conquesting, still unrested in the spiritual realm.

The karmic tie between the client and Alexander wasn't through direct warfare—but through royal agreements and decrees signed in alignment with conquest. Even passive support, in this case, carried immense karmic weight.

This created spiritual binds that entangled the client in residual energies of conquest, war, and power.

Clearing the Echoes of War

This session required deep karmic healing—perhaps more than any war timeline I've witnessed:

» Deceit and manipulation of kingdoms

» Betrayals between rulers

» The overtaking of armies

» Entire villages slain to uncover secrets of other cities

» Brutality masked as strategy

I spent over 30 minutes in energetic repair—cleansing lands, washing fields of battle, healing villages, and calling back every lost soul still stuck in that field.

The Crossing & Final Peace

The final step was crossing over the souls—but it wasn't immediate.

These souls were so weighed down that Earth's guardians had to be summoned to cleanse their consciousness before they could even begin their crossing.

When it was done, the feeling was immense.

The biggest release I've ever witnessed.

Now, for the first time, Alexander the Great was at peace.

So are all those who fought, who fell, and who carried the pain of that timeline for centuries.

What a gift to Gaia.

Witnessing a war timeline like this, healed and transmuted, is something I will never forget.

A Fabulous Past Life in Sirius

A 1-1 Session Story

I simply had to share this one.

In this session, we entered one of the most magnificent lifetimes I've ever witnessed—a breathtaking soul memory from Sirius, filled with advanced technology, deep emotion, ancient ceremonies, and galactic-level purpose.

The Speed Horses & The Ceremony Begins

It all began on Sirius, with the client arriving to perform a sacred Sirian ceremony. To get to the first site, she rode what can be described as speed horses—creatures faster than Earth's fastest vehicles, capable of reaching distant mountain ranges in seconds.

Her first destination? The Leap of Faith.

The 1000-Meter Dive & The Vision in Freefall

Part of the Sirian ceremony involved leaping from a 1,000-meter cliff into the crystal waters below. This "freefall" experience was designed to simulate a near-death state—bringing visions, clarity, and spiritual downloads.

To survive the fall safely, liquid energy spheres were placed over the body, acting like a shield to prevent physical damage from impact. But here's where it got amazing:

During the fall—just seconds in Earth time—we spent 15 minutes in the visions.

A Visit from Her Sister

The first vision? Her younger sister, who had passed in this life.

She appeared instantly, glowing with joy and love. She told the client:

"I've never left. I'm with Mom. I watch over the cousins. I fly as a bird for fun sometimes. I'm still here."

The love was palpable.

Then, she said:

"Come—I want to show you something."

And just like that, we were pulled into a past life memory...

The Scientist Who Saved Sirius

The client, in a past incarnation, was a Sirian scientist. She discovered the original star they were living on was going to explode. Knowing this, she helped lead a mass planetary evacuation.

45% of the planet agreed to leave.

55% stayed behind, accepting their fate.

They stargated through the oceans of what we now call Sirius, entering a shielded underwater civilization, not in water—but beneath it, hidden from the surface world. From here, they integrated slowly with life, monitoring and planning.

The client later returned to the destroyed planet and rescued survivors who had gone underground.

Among them was a famous Sirian being—one connected to Earth's ancient programs and seen in Hindu scriptures. (Yes, that well-known.)

The moment before she hit the water... gave us the full origin of the Sirian guardians and how the client played a role in saving Sirius itself.

The Mission of the Sirians

We were reminded how crucial the Sirians are in our current ascension.

Had they not survived, who would be watching Earth from above now?

Today, the Sirians serve as universal peacekeepers, tracking asteroids, extinction threats, and planetary collapses. They operate at all levels with fail-safe backup systems. They are the galactic guardians of life.

And this client?

She was the reason they made it.

The Mountain Masters of Sirius

After this breathtaking ceremony, the client was taken high into the Sirian mountains where—yes, even on Sirius—the masters live in the mountains.

She met three masters:

The first master brought forward her future child—a soul from another universe. He gave her details that were important for her to one day share with her child, so he would remember who he truly is.

The other two masters greeted her in a cenote as mermaids, laughing and swimming with joy at her arrival.

What followed was weeks of connection, deep heart-to-heart talks, soul reflection, guidance, and support.

They listened to her entire life story with full presence and responded with divine love—until everything was understood and healed.

By the end, it was like reuniting with lifelong best friends in the most beautiful way imaginable.

Final Reflections

What a session. What a soul.

This journey to Sirius was filled with technological beauty, deep healing, soul reunions, and galactic history.

To witness someone who once saved a race now returning to awaken her memories and receive new light codes is one of the greatest honors.

We are truly in the era of remembrance.

And this session proves it.

The Lost Story of the Arc of the Covenant

As revealed through past-life recall and divine channeling.

Many theories exist about the true nature of the Arc of the Covenant.

Some say it holds all knowledge. Others claim it's the power of God itself.

Its origin has been debated across centuries—tied to Israel, Egypt, and beyond.

But in my personal experiences—through past-life 1-on-1 sessions and deep channeling—the Arc has now come forward three times, each with growing clarity.

The Glimpse with Yeshua

In one vision, Yeshua, during his travels to Egypt, came across the Arc.

He recognized a powerful Source light within it, yet the full story did not reveal itself—until this session.

The Arc, the Sisterhood, and the Sky Gods

In this 1-on-1 session, a powerful memory emerged.

The Arc was revealed to have been created by the Sisterhood of the Rose, working in sacred alliance with the Sky Gods. It was not merely a container but a living divine technology—etched within it was the God Light Language, a celestial script holding the codes of the gods.

These weren't just visual inscriptions. They were living frequencies.

When tuned into, these codes do something extraordinary:

They purify your God Consciousness.

I don't say that lightly.

Having worked extensively with the vibration of God Consciousness, I felt it in every part of my being—the codes from the Arc create a literal purification of the divine self.

The Arc's Role in Atlantis & Egypt

The client in the session had an Atlantean lifetime where she was a conduit between the God Realms and Earth.

Together, she and the Sky Gods created the Arc to preserve the divine connection within the Earth realms.

Its first mission was to serve the royal bloodlines of light—those who held the Christ lineage in both Atlantis and Egypt. It was eventually brought to Egypt and safeguarded by the pharaonic families.

But its magic was subtle and sacred.

When one of the royal lineages lost faith or veered from divine connection,

they would gaze into the golden codes within the Arc.

And just like that—

they would remember.

"This divinity that you seek outside...

is what you truly are."

The Arc restored the memory of God within.

Not through dogma or fear—but by igniting the remembrance of one's eternal light.

A Divine Integration.

As the session came to its apex, something incredible happened.

A flash of light appeared behind the client.

An ascended master entered the space, bringing radiant support.

It was then revealed—

this client was one of the original creators of the Arc,

working with the Sky Gods during the ancient golden age.

Now, in this life, she was ready to reintegrate that energy,

to once again embody the codes of divinity,

and assist others in doing the same.

Final Reflection

The Arc was never meant to be lost.

Its true essence was never just in its physical form.

It was—and still is—a mirror of God Consciousness for those ready to remember.

And in these times of great awakening,

it is returning.

Through those who created it. Through those who carry its codes. Through you.

Healing in the In-Between Dimensions: My Most Expanded Session Yet

During a 1-1 session, the client's Higher Self looked at me and said:

"I want you to work in-between my dimensions of self."

I paused.

"I've never done that before," I admitted.

He smiled:

"It's time for you to expand your healings."

And so began one of the most profound healing journeys I've ever facilitated.

Understanding the In-Between Dimensions

To offer perspective:

The in-between dimension of Earth is like a subfloor basement—a hidden support layer that feeds energy into portals of the quantum grids that rise into our experience of Earth. It's coded architecture beneath the known, something I had only previously entered alongside Yeshua when he showed me the layered in-betweens of Gaia herself.

To even begin healing at this level, you must understand the full ladder of consciousness—all levels, their function, and how they interconnect.

This is the very foundation of the Unity Series I channeled.

So I anchored in, braced for depth, and began.

Starting at Prime Source

I began at the top—Prime Source within the client.

What I saw shocked me: vast, endless space. Stars. Silence.

I asked, "Why is there so much space?"

His higher self answered:

"Because there is so much space. Everywhere."

Then I was shown the Oversoul Oneness wanting to integrate. This would bring the client into deeper alignment with their higher I AM presence.

Meeting the Infinite Teams of Light Moving downward, I encountered a council team stationed just below the client's Prime Source.

I asked, "Who are you?"

"We are his Infinite Teams of Light," they said.

"We've guided his ascension across lifetimes—but when a soul says 'no' to guidance, disconnections form."

To repair this, we opened his Akashic Records and cleared every moment where he had unconsciously said no to his divine teams.

Immediately, we began reigniting the connections between him and his full dimensional support network.

The Alpha Omega Consciousness

Then we entered the Alpha Omega level, the first level of fragmentation.

Here, I saw 10,000+ fragments of his original light, all sent out to experience different realities. These fragmented further into millions, billions, trillions, all the way to zillions—each one diving deeper into density, further away from Oneness.

Our task:

Reconnect his full I AM Oneness with every single zillionth-level fragment.

It took time—but the reconnection was complete.

Rewriting God Consciousness Modules

Then we came to the God Consciousness field—and what I saw blew my mind.

Here, I was shown how the gods created the first levels of density simulations—modules designed to carry experiences of separation.

This is where "not-love" first appears, a stark contrast to all higher levels which are of pure love.

Our instructions:

Clear the mark of the gods on the outdated simulation modules

Call upon the Councils of Deletion

Delete the old programs

Recreate new love-based modules to anchor into Earth's grids

I asked, "Who are the Councils of Deletion?"

They appeared—white light master coders of the universe.

They input anti-code, causing the simulation to dissolve itself from within.

Absolutely remarkable.

Crystalline Source & Guilt Release

Finally, we arrived at the Crystalline Source.

Here, a deep guilt consciousness emerged from a past life.

We worked through it and released it fully.

The emotional liberation was immense. The field shifted completely.

Final Reflection

This session was unlike anything I've ever done.

I witnessed how the in-between dimensions serve as the scaffolding for all the source-level constructs we engage with.

They are living blueprints that hold the structure for our multi-dimensional self.

When healed, they allow for full integration of Oneness into the human form.

To say I'm grateful doesn't fully express my gratitude.

This session was a masterclass in healing architecture, in source mechanics, and in the sheer grace of what's possible.

We are integrating more than we know.

And now, the bridges between dimensions... are opening.

The Tree Aspect & the Cosmic Angel: A Session I'll Never Forget

It's truly fascinating to witness things you've never seen before in 1-1 sessions.

Today, something incredibly unique happened:

A tree aspect of the client came forward.

She explained that she had once been a tree, and it made perfect sense—her groundedness, her stability, and the way she serves as a pillar for others. She's deeply rooted in life, in truth, and in being. Then, she shared one of the most incredible healing techniques I've ever encountered. Out of respect for her divine gift, I won't share it here. But trust me—it was otherworldly.

I've spoken with trees before. I know their wisdom. But this was the first time a tree aspect of a soul came through in such clarity.

 Next, it got even more extraordinary.

A cosmic angel arrived.

Not just any angel—but a teacher angel who guides planets across the entire multiverse.

She's not just here for Earth—she teaches from direct experience, from lives lived, from mastery attained.

Her love frequency?

Beyond golden source.

Beyond what I thought possible.

This cosmic angel merged with the client—an aspect of her higher self—to upgrade her entire love frequency. The love she radiated was unreal. The purest joy-love, overflowing with unconditional acceptance and radiant healing.

It touched every cell in the session.

It touched me.

This is the age of the masters.

So many of you are waking up to your vastness.

You are cosmic teachers, tree healers, planetary guides, angelic frequencies incarnate.

To work with you is the greatest honor.

You're not just remembering who you are—you're anchoring it.

I'm here in reverence.

We are not alone.

We are not small.

We are ready.

Children of the Light—A 1-on-1 Session That Changed Everything

Such an incredible 1-1 session today.

It was clear this was going to be something special from the very first moment.

The client was instantly connected to three radiant streams of light:

10,000+ angels, Her guide teams, and her higher healer aspects—the lifetimes where she served as a divine healer. Suddenly, her guides stepped forward—and with them was Mother Mary and, surprisingly,

Saint Joseph. His presence was deeply significant as I've only seen Joseph once in all my years of doing this work.

Then came the vision...

They brought us back to a lifetime during Yeshua's time.

She was healing hearts, even bringing a man back to life.

As a young girl, she wandered forests, talking to elementals and receiving powerful psychic visions—some of the future, others remote viewing moments from across the world.

As she matured, we were taken to a scene outside a home, sitting in a circle with Yeshua and Magdalene. I was there too.

We were meditating together, building an immense light field to initiate children who reached the age of activation.

These sacred initiations were standard in that timeline—preparing children for their divine path by awakening their higher streams and connecting them to source, light, and love.

Then it happened...

We brought our awareness to the now.

We called in that same Christ field and initiated children across the world.

Her legion of angels traveled across Earth, visiting children, healing trauma, and restoring joy to their hearts—especially to those who suffered through the density of parental pain or early hardship.

And then I saw it...

Laughter echoing through homes.

Joy rising in the hearts of children.

Light filling every space.

The entire planetary consciousness shifted.

The voices of the children rang out,

and through them, joy touched every home.

Yeshua said it best:

"The children are the key."

It's why they were the focus of activations in his time.

And it's why they will be the focus again.

Together with this amazing soul, I'll be announcing Light Missions for Children soon.

If you feel the call to bring light to Earth's children,

to heal, uplift, and help them remember who they are...

Stay tuned.

We'll be inviting many of you to join.

The Children of the Light are rising.

And we're going to meet them there.

The Oracles of Atlantis & The Healers of the Great Fall

In today's 1-1 session, something ancient was remembered.

The client was revealed to be one of three great Oracles—originally from Lemuria—who held sacred positions within the Atlantean Tower at the city center, maintaining the light grids of Atlantis during its final days.

As the great fall began, these three were the last to stand, holding the divine records and keeping the higher dimensions of light open with every ounce of energy they could summon.

The Great Threat

The fall wasn't just a collapse of civilization.

The fall was the rise of the false matrix—the creation of the lower 4th dimension, a realm of distortion and density (now dismantled in our current timeline).

Through intricate coding, reptilian and draconian forces engineered this realm—implanting a dark grid infrastructure that unleashed swarms of demonic entities. These waves of distortion tore through the Earth field, forming a barrier between Gaia and the higher realms of light.

The Oracles couldn't stop the seal.

The atmosphere was cloaked.

Gaia was cut off, and the light became unreachable.

Divine Recovery

At the beginning of the session, Yeshua appeared—guiding me to extract the Oracle's light and the Atlantean records from the fallen timeline.

Once outside of it, we began re-coding the timeline:

Dissolving the density.

Healing the hearts of the collective who had suffered in the fall.

Retrieving stuck souls still bound to the event.

Reclaiming the Pillars

It was then revealed that the reptilian beings had created a dark pillar—a stream of black light descending from their feet into the lowest realms, connecting directly to the beast of darkness that fueled this false construct.

In an act of divine alchemy, we re-coded their dark pillars into light, sending high frequencies down into the deepest realms—healing countless trapped souls and reversing the polarity of the darkness from within.

The Oracle's Return

At the close of the session, the client reclaimed her right of power, performing a divine ceremony to reconnect with the other two Oracles.

This activated a field unseen for millennia—an luminous Field of Universal Consciousness—anchored now through her, and accessible to all beings on Gaia ready to receive.

The Oracles have returned.

The ancient records are safe.

The healing of Atlantis has begun.

The Planet of Love: Jalibu

In a recent 1-1 session, the client brought us into the frequency of a Pleiadian planet called Jalibu (or Yalibu)—known as the Planet of Love.

On this planet, the telepathy between the sea kingdoms and land beings had evolved into full harmony. All ecosystems worked together consciously, exchanging love and awareness as one planetary field. The planetary consciousness itself had reached a level where all life was in divine cooperation.

The Sacred Temple of Light

The client had spent many lifetimes in a sacred holy temple—a place equivalent in frequency to what Lemuria is to us on Earth. Upon entering the temple, it appeared like a crystalline fortress—vast and open, like a massive cave with a high ceiling where light poured in. Inside were ascended teams of light whose only task was to lovingly help align your energy field as you entered.

Chamber of Return

In the next area was the Convergence Room—a frequency chamber designed to gather scattered consciousness and bring your soul and energy fully back into Self. This was essential to prepare for what came next.

Chamber of Clarity (A Message for All)

This room was strongly emphasized by the higher teams as one of the most important areas.

In this space, you are asked to meditate on three sacred questions:

What can I do more to assist my Divine Self?

What can I do more to assist with the Divine Plan?

What can I do more to assist this Divine Planet?

The message was clear: if everyone on Earth meditated deeply and consistently on these three questions, life would become incredibly magical and aligned.

Galactic Co-Creation Chamber

Finally, the client was brought into a chamber where she connected with all of her galactic teams.

Here, a deep truth was revealed:

"When people say, the Universe will support you, it's not the vague 'universe'—it's your light teams, your galactic family, consciously co-creating with you in real time."

In this sacred space, she sat with her teams and telepathically communicated her ideas, dreams, and choices. They in turn offered their point of view, and together they co-created reality across dimensions.

This session was a profound blessing—a glimpse into what true planetary and galactic harmony looks like.

Jalibu is real. The frequency of divine collaboration is real.

And the invitation is now open to align with it.

The Tall Whites & Earth's Environmental Origins

I've only heard a few stories about the Tall Whites (and those were many years ago).

In all of my sessions and countless journeys through the Akashic Records, I never once saw them—until this session.

Environmental Engineers from the Stars

The Tall Whites appeared during a pre-Lemurian timeline, present on a remote island off the coast between Europe and Asia.

They were bio-scientists—not here for conquest or study, but with a divine mission:

to restore environmental harmony and enhance life-sustaining ecosystems on Earth.

They worked hand-in-hand with some of the earliest humans. These humans were pure, light-filled, and untouched by corruption—truly in unity consciousness. Together, the Tall Whites and these humans initiated environmental programming and engineering projects meant to stabilize planetary ecosystems and ensure Gaia's abundance.

The Departure & the Collective Wound

After a long phase of work and testing, the Tall Whites began preparing for their departure, giving the humans an entire year (by our calendar) to adjust and prepare.

Here is where the client's personal role was revealed:

She had been the lead environmental engineer working closely with the Tall Whites. Upon their departure, she was entrusted with continuing their mission using some of the foundational technologies they left behind.

But something tragic occurred. The humans began to lose interest.

Without the presence of the star beings, they started to believe the mission was no longer important. They stopped listening to her.

They dismissed her role, saying she was not "special" and didn't have the authority to lead anymore.

This became a deep wound of abandonment for the client—but more importantly, it exposed a collective wound in humanity itself:

A moment in our shared history where we chose to stop caring for Mother Earth.

A consciousness fracture where humanity turned away from environmental stewardship.

Healing the Break

Through the session, we addressed this forgotten fracture and began healing the collective wound—restoring the memory and importance of actively caring for Gaia.

The work the client did allowed a reconnection in the grids to humanity's environmental mission.

By healing this ancient wound, we made it easier for humanity to:

Re-establish deep heart connection to Gaia,

Prioritize the balance of ecosystems,

Develop new conscious technologies for monitoring and protecting Earth,

And recommit to living in harmony with nature.

This healing set a powerful tone for our planetary future.

The Return of the Great Star Families

This session revealed an early origin story of the Tall Whites—one of the great star families that supported the evolution of humanity. As we know from Lemurian teachings, Earth was never alone. Earth was always guided and uplifted by interstellar allies.

And now, as the shift approaches, it feels inevitable:

They will return.

To celebrate.

To reunite.

To witness humanity rise again.

A God Among Us: The Origin of a Master Soul

There are certain 1-1 sessions I will never forget.

This was one of them.

The origins of a soul can be vast—spanning realms, lifetimes, and even entire universes. But this soul... was exceptional. She didn't just originate from another star system—she came from many universes over, as a god being of full power.

The Eternal Guardian

She was a guardian over countless species and realms—a most

trusted eternal being with infinite gifts. She could hold a sun in her hands and speak through it, her words vibrating across the stars to other god beings. She embodied the voice of divinity, channeling frequency through celestial fire.

But what happens when you've been powerful for eons?

Even immortality grows weary.

One day, she stood before the other god beings of her universal structure and declared:

"I want to begin again. I want to forget my power...and remember it, one step at a time."

In an act of absolute surrender, she turned into light. Her immortal form dissolved, and she streamed herself through the sun with the other god beings, entering our universal structure.

Her First Incarnation: Sirius A

Her journey began on Sirius A.

She incarnated as a blue being with a tall cone-shaped head, navigating the skies with strange air-based technology—not quite a ship, but a frequency-hovering vessel. This technology amplified her telepathy and helped her communicate directly with the Sky Gods she once served beside.

In this life, she helped with the Stargate Program—receiving alignment instructions from the Sky Gods to rebalance frequency distortions. She soared above oceans and cities in direct service to the celestial order.

The Bio-Key Revelation

Then came the revelation.

One of her past aspects carried something extraordinary—

something hidden until now:

A bio-key.

This bio-key wasn't just personal—it was planetary. It unlocked a biofield of intelligent awareness, designed to block the influence of archon frequencies on the Master and God Consciousness fields of Earth.

Let that sink in.

This key was released to the collective during this session.

It was the first bio-key I ever witnessed with such intelligent awareness—an evolutionary frequency that supports the entire collective by:

Shielding the highest fields of awakening,

Restoring divine clarity,

And removing distortions that have long interfered with soul remembrance.

And with it...

Many will awaken.

Many will remember their truth.

Many will rise into their divine mastery—without a shadow holding them back.

This was a powerful, sacred session.

A reminder that some souls don't come here to learn.

They come here to reignite the divine design.

She did just that.

The Most Profound 1-on-1 Session I've Been Honoured to Facilitate

Many of you know my deep connection to Sirius, where I received my master's training in this universal structure. While I feel like a pupil among the stars—equal to all beings of light—my heart has always been magnetically tied to the Sirian realms. They visited me throughout this life, and this session reminded me why that bond is so sacred.

What unfolded was not only unexpected...

it was divinely orchestrated.

The Sirian Royal Temple of Earth

Guided by Yeshua, I was taken up into the light and instructed to follow a specific frequency—to the client's first Earth incarnation.

What I saw was incredible.

There stood a blue-skinned Sirian being of immense power and majesty, radiating blessings of light and wisdom to waves of galactic beings who were beaming into an ancient Earth temple.

This temple wasn't just sacred—it was a universal hub. Her ship, stationed in the cosmos, was being used as a frequency transponder, transmitting a vibration of trust. This allowed beings from other star systems to teleport between universes and arrive directly at this Earth-based station of light.

Each time one arrived, she blessed them—and telepathically transmitted instructions about Earth's dimensional layers and how they could assist in the formation of the planet's light infrastructure.

Yeshua whispered,

"She is Sirian royalty."

Instantly, I knew—this was the first incarnated Sirian Queen I ever encountered on Earth.

The 12 Tribes and Seeding of Guardian Souls

We followed her story forward...

What we saw next left me speechless.

There were humans not from Earth, ancient light beings from distant systems. Together, they birthed a project—one I'd only heard whispers of in distant records.

Through genetic coding and frequency alignment, they magnetized souls of the highest love into specially prepared wombs. This wasn't just birth... this was divine soul engineering.

This process created what became the:

12 Galactic Hybrids

12 Earth Guardian Tribes

12 Founding Races of Illumination

These beings would serve as the eternal protectors of Earth, holding the light during humanity's darkest hours, anchoring ascension codes, and carrying out Gaia's divine plan across eons of time.

It was she—this Sirian master—who initiated this program.

The Lemurian Reincarnation & Galactic Royalty

Later, she programmed her own reincarnation timeline to ensure her consciousness would return during Lemuria.

There, she joined a circle of Galactic Royal Incarnates, including Pleiadian royalty and 10 other sovereign light beings. They rejoiced in the innocent joy and divine play of Lemurian life before their eventual retreat into Inner Earth.

Yeshua then showed us how this same royal Sirian being—the client—is now reconnecting in our timeline, bringing her full teams of light into alignment. We witnessed an explosion of love frequencies as her presence reawakened these ancient alliances across Gaia.

The Crown Jewel: Training Yeshua in Egypt

Then came the most sacred revelation of all.

Yeshua revealed a timeline where she was one of his teachers in ancient Egypt.

An Ascended Master in full form, she trained him in frequency mastery—but more than that, she showed him who he was.

She told him:

"You are the very Heart of God incarnate.

You are the living pulse of the Mother-Father God's core love."

She explained something that moved me to my core.

The Mother-Father God consciousness, while infinite and unknowable, has a center—a heart center—that is the purest pulse of divine love in all existence. And Yeshua is the living embodiment of that pulse.

He is the catalyst of planetary love, the one called upon by all galactic councils to bless Earth with the core heart frequency that restores all beings to their origin: Love.

And she—this Sirian master—is from that same core heart energy.

Together, in our session, they merged timelines and brought this frequency into Gaia.

I felt the wave.

I know many of you will too.

A Final Reflection

It's wild to think...

Some people go through life believing they're just "average."

But then you see who they truly are in the Akashic records...

And it changes everything.

If this is you—

If you're reading this and wondering if you could be royalty, ancient, cosmic, divine—

Let me tell you:

You already are.

You're just remembering now.

This... is only the beginning.

A Hidden Memory of Yeshua at Age 6—A Sacred 1-on-1 Session

In this session, I experienced one of the most heart-opening journeys I've ever had the honor of facilitating.

Yeshua came forward with a gentle, radiant presence. He created a sacred field of light forming a high-frequency space for us to connect in. With such love in his eyes, he said:

"I want to share a memory that no one knows."

The client and I sat with him ethereally, and we were instantly transported into a living memory—a moment from when Yeshua was only six years old.

The Rock by the Ocean

We saw him sitting on a large sun-warmed rock, overlooking the vast ocean. The waves were soft and rhythmic... sacred. The light shimmered around him, and the air held a stillness that felt eternal.

Then, a female angel appeared.

With grace beyond words, she invited him into the heavenly realm—not in body, but in light. At just six years old, Yeshua's third eye was fully open. He could see it all.

One by one, the angels of heaven arrived.

Each introduced themselves, and gently merged their fields with his in absolute love, bliss, and celestial union. The atmosphere was saturated with peace and eternity.

And then, something extraordinary happened.

His Angelic Self Appeared

His angelic self—the higher essence of who he is—came forward.

"We are the same,"

it said.

"There is no separation—only one of us walks in heaven, and one of us walks on Earth."

With that said, the angelic self merged with Yeshua's six-year-old form.

A brilliant light ignited within him. We saw his energy rise through many levels of divine light, anchoring something profound—the knowing of his path.

In this moment, he was told his purpose:

To release humanity of their sins,

To awaken the Sacred Heart,

And to open the path of ascension for all.

This moment gave Yeshua an unshakable peace and bliss—a

knowing that lived deep in his heart from that age forward.

The Gift to the Client: Ascending Everything

Then, Yeshua turned to the client with so much love in his eyes.

He brought her awareness into her infinite self—

All universes, all galaxies, all stars, all beings—

And gently said:

"Feel everything within you ascend.

Give all the hearts what they need to release.

Let all be healed—

for that is what is required to ascend."

She became the cosmic womb of love, transmitting healing to every soul, star, and strand of light across her infinite expression.

A Triumph of the Light

Five hours after the session ended,

I was still in a state of pure bliss.

There are some moments you don't just experience.

You savor them.

You honor them.

You let them live in your heart forever.

This was one of them.

Sometimes, you simply and humbly bow...

in awe of the triumph of the light.

The Halo Serum: A Galactic Discovery That Sparked Interstellar Peace

1-1 Session Download

What an extraordinary session this was—truly one of the most advanced star-level transmissions I've ever witnessed.

It all began on Lyra during a high-level interstellar meeting between the Lyrans and a delegation of Pleiadians who recently returned from an incredible discovery.

A Planet of Pure Heart Vibration

The Pleiadians found a planet unlike any other—not technologically advanced but radiating with the purest heart-based frequency. The lifeforms on this world lived in such high vibrational coherence that disease didn't exist. They carefully extracted a golden serum from this world, storing it in containment drums aboard their ship. The human word that came through for this incredible substance was:

"Halo."

This was not just a healing serum—it was a consciousness amplifier rooted in the vibration of pure love and inner harmony.

A New Proposal: Healing the Rogue

As the Pleiadians shared their findings with the Lyrans, including holographic visuals of the planet, its species, and the biofield analytics, an idea formed.

The Lyrans had rehabilitation programs for those who had gone rogue—beings who had committed acts of harm or violence. They proposed using the Halo serum in these cases.

We focused on patient 1, a Lyran who killed his sister in a fit of rage as a young being. Traditionally, when introduced to simulations involving his sister in the Lyran Holodeck (a consciousness-responsive healing simulator), he would spiral into depression or self-hatred.

But after ingesting Halo...

Something miraculous happened.

When his sister appeared in the hologram—she hugged him.

Instant forgiveness.

Pure love.

The simulation, being consciousness-sensitive, reflected this higher healing state. The Lyran rehabilitation team watched in awe as remorse, depression, and trauma left his body at staggering rates. It was the most rapid transformation they ever saw.

The Interstellar Cooperation Ship

The client's Lyran aspect then began assisting in the distribution of Halo across star systems.

We were transported to a massive interstellar civilization ship, a galactic collaboration hub where dozens of star races were working together to understand Halo's full potential.

Then—something incredible.

The ship began to communicate directly with me in binary code.

My thumb and finger started tapping out binary sequences—the first time this has ever happened in a session.

As I tuned in, the ship showed me:

Its voyages through space and time,

How they embedded Halo into foods, drinks, and even frequencies,

How they found ways to encode it into DNA strands, healing ancestral lines,

And how this catalyzed interstellar peace between formerly conflicting civilizations.

Halo was more than a serum—it was a frequency of unified consciousness, and it changed everything.

Final Activation: Earth Receives the Codes

To close the session, we were guided to download the codes of the Halo serum into the Earth's energetic grid. We sent it through the DNA of all beings, to assist in deep healing and soul remembrance.

You may not see it with your eyes—but the light of Halo is already flowing.

This session was a revelation.

A testament to how one pure vibration of love—shared with humility, respect, and intention—can change the trajectory of entire civilizations.

And that time… is now.

The Elvin Kingdoms: Stories Never Told

There are some stories hidden so deeply in the folds of time that only the heart can remember them… until they are revealed again through the soul.

In two 1-on-1 sessions with a beautiful couple, a door opened into the long-lost mysteries of the Elvin Kingdoms—what was revealed brought ancient magic back into view.

Forgotten Allies of Light,

Throughout my journey, I always wondered about the Elvin realms— beings spoken of in ancient folklore yet absent from most spiritual teachings.

Then, one day, they started appearing in sessions.

I began meeting them and remembering them.

They were present with Yeshua during the time of the Essenes, present during the time of Lemuria, and were key stewards of high-frequency light on Earth.

Their great portals allowed them to travel through dimensions, and they played a vital role in the advancement of consciousness on this planet—a role that was forgotten... until now.

The Hidden Portal

There is one Elvin portal I've long known—guarded for ages by the beings I call the men in black. Their presence kept the frequency low, preventing access. But in a pivotal moment during a session, we cleared them.

When we did—something magical happened.

The portal opened into Inner Earth, revealing one of the Elvin Kingdoms.

It is truly breathtaking.

Only those with a high enough frequency can access it, and while I cannot share the entry point publicly (as there are still risks), I can say:

It exists.

And it is sacred.

The Couple & The Elvin Universe

In these two profound sessions, the couple's past-life revelations activated ancient timelines and gifts for the collective.

The husband held a rare Elvin aspect—but not from this universe.

He brought in a magical frequency of abundance, seeded from a parallel Elvin realm.

We activated it, and it flowed outward to benefit the entire Earth field.

Then came his wife's session—and with it, one of the most incredible Elvin stories I've ever witnessed.

The Elvin Scrolls & The War Across Five Planets

She was once a powerful Elvin guardian—not only of a kingdom but of five Elvin planets.

In the age of separation, when the one who turned from God created monsters of anti-light, those dark forces invaded the Elvin systems. They sought to sever the Elves from their divine language, memory, and power.

What she did next was heroic:

She gathered all the gold-embroidered Elvin scrolls, written in the ancient Elvin tongue, and traveled from planet to planet—reminding the Elvin beings of who they were.

The Elvin language is not just words, it is light code.

When spoken, it activates protection, memory, and divine clarity.

It began clearing the darkness and entire planets were saved.

But not all.

One planet fell.

That planet... was Earth.

The Retreat to Inner Earth

Just as Lemuria and Agartha withdrew into the Earth during the great fall, so too did the Elvin Kingdoms. Their portals were sealed and hidden, but their presence remained—for those who remember and hold the frequency of love, light, and magic.

The Elves are not fantasy.

They are living beings of light, wisdom, and enchantment—and they are returning.

Welcoming the Elves Once More

So to the Elvin Kingdoms:

We remember you.

We honor your sacrifice.

And we welcome you back into our timelines, into our hearts, and into the New Earth.

Your magic, your beauty, your songs of divine remembrance are deeply needed now.

Thank you for staying with us—even when the world forgot.

PART IV

PUBLIC
CHANNELINGS

PART IV: MY PUBLIC CHANNELINGS

As a starseed activator and channeler, I've always felt a deep responsibility to serve the collective during this pivotal time on Earth. Channeling divine councils, galactic guides, and higher-dimensional beings has become an essential part of my mission—to assist fellow starseeds in understanding the ascension process, the shifts in Earth's frequency, and the greater trajectory of our collective evolution.

These channelings offer insight into how divine realms support Earth's consciousness awakening and provide clarity to those navigating their spiritual path. It felt important to include some of these transmissions in this book so readers gain a deeper understanding of the councils and the guides that walk with us—and hear, in their own words, the messages they've shared to uplift and activate humanity.

The Ministries of Heaven

A channeling from Yeshua.

"Greetings beloved children, brothers, sisters, friends.

We sit together in the ministries of heaven while you sleep.

You have come from all time, all frequencies, all universes, all realities to Earth to bring peace where there is discord, love where there is sadness, hope where there is none. To lift up, to let go, to rise above the temptations of the Luciferian agenda that keeps Earth suppressed and the divine voice dormant. For you are the holders and keepers of faith, the family of light of the highest orders that will complete the divine plan as it was promised and foretold.

I praise you all for overcoming all that you have. You have triumphed over abuse, public humiliation, being ridiculed, shamed, abused, and hurt. Yet you rise again, you hold true to your heart, you hold peace in your knowing, and trust in the dreams of dreams to come. So many of you have faced the greatest adversities and yet you continue to find a way through, to believe and keep your faith strong.

It is for this I praise you and I share some good news. The choirs of angels now sing to the collective heart of the day to come that was foretold and promised. As they sing, no heart can remain asleep. The song is of the completion of the divine plan, of the ascension of heaven on Earth. It is the song now being sung to all souls on Earth and its eternities of timelines. As the hearts hear this, the mass awakening surges, and all hearts that were closed are now awake. For they have heard the voice of God, the heavenly Father and Mother through the choirs of angels that now sing the divine song.

The ministries of heaven will continue, and you will continue to see me until the day when I return. I will come from the heavens, not in judgment but in acceptance, not in punishment but in welcoming, not in anger but in love. For I hold the keys to heaven, and on this day, the day that is to come, the day that has been foretold, I will be welcoming all to heaven on Earth. This is the day of the ascension."

St Germain on the Ascension Currently

"The ending of tyranny has begun.

It is to understand it as cycles, and as anger has a cycle so does hate, as does violence. These things must end as the heart awakening happening is opening, and as it opens the requirement for energy in consciousness changes. Before the awakening, the energy was in a closed heart loop system, and in a closed system of fear, division and war can thrive as the energy in a closed heart system feeds this energy source as a collective energy. When the system opens as an open heart system, the energy requirement changes to a new energy that is needed. Thus the energy shifts and the reality changes as cycles end and new circuits become active in the collective heart and mind.

It is easy to explain then as you are underway of the greatest heart opening in 2025 that has ever occurred on Earth. As the requirements of the collective changes, new circles and new government bodies have to form to support the new collective heart requirements of an open heart-based system.

The current reforms in society will reflect this new energetic need, such as transparency and openness. Heart-centric unity will proceed from these, and bring the eventuality of peace on Earth.

The nebula cosmic light coming through is also from a higher cosmic council due to the readiness of those on Earth to receive it. This will lead to a new supportive cosmic alliance opening for contact and higher dimensional beings as this is the desired frequency to experience during an open-heart society.

I am very pleased to share that great changes are advancing even greater changes, both consciously and in how you will experience your reality, as the open-heart system emerges in the collective consciousness in the year 2025."

A Channeled Message From the Councils of Christ

"Greetings beloved souls,

Now we sit in the aisle of destiny.

Our service is to your heart. We are here to assist your wildest dreams as you sit and ponder in new belief systems.

We are here to address the situational mass awakening occurring in the year 2025 and what this means for you.

The Council of Dreams are diligently working to bring hope, prosperity, and ideals of love to the waking masses.

Our aim is to bring forth a new relationship to the dreaming and waking world, uniting a consciousness that has remained silent for many.

The purpose of this driven effort is to bring peace to the internal worlds of the collective heart.

We look to clear the chaos of the mind; the arguments of the internal dilemmas all are facing, so they can find solitude to the questions within.

The subconsciousness is beginning to let go so the higher self can flow and direct a more aligned love-based outcome by resolving the internal worlds, by bringing dreams of conflicts within, or dilemmas of their life, to find resolution and solace.

As the collective leaps in these months ahead, so will their awareness. As their awareness grows within self, they too shall find answers intuitively beyond the veil and begin to realize they are awakened. During this awakening at grand scale, it will open new awareness in the collective's unity heart bringing hope to many causes and conflicts to which solutions will be intuitively manifested by teams of love guiding all towards peace and unity.

This is forward consciousness. As the consciousness grows and expands across the mass awakening that is underway, the lightworker community will advance beyond their previous incarnations on Earth as humans. They will feel a renewed faith in the divine dream being realized as they too will be guided to great peace within. The feelings will grow collectively and be felt by all. It is different now in this mass awakening than anything you have experienced before. New alignments, new hope, and easier connections that bring you to the forefront of your abundance will be realized as all are becoming synchronized consciously into the divine plan of the ascension.

From an awareness of those who have been pushing the boundaries of consciousness, you will feel a great lift up, a boost in happiness, love creation, and demand for your offerings as the synchronization through the collective awakening will increase and align to the divine plan that you are creating in to assist those that need to find you. A need is greater than a want. It is a driving force, and as the higher selves take a more flow state through dream state and awakened guidance, all will become synced to the alignment in need to find the answers to the greatest awakening that has ever occurred in all of humanities' versions and timelines for themselves and their divinity.

In parting,

The Councils of Christ understand it has not been easy to advance with such adversity. But you have, and now you will find a greater flow, a deeper synchronization allowing your frequencies to rise even greater and with ease. The guide teams will come to you more often with messages to assist your divine dream that is in alignment and synced to the collective during the great leap forward in consciousness you will experience in 2025."

A Message from the Great Mother Sophia Christ

"Don't ever accept yourself as being unhappy. It means there are some adjustments you need to make.

Don't ever leave behind the destiny in your heart.

Feel into the source of your love and let it grow within you.

The bearers of bad news are the deliveries of the good. For they are delivering you a chance to find more love inside.

Find yourself on the ascension councils and choose your path towards enlightenment. Do not ever stop dreaming about completing your divine plan.

Do not ever say no to your divine dream.

Many face fears and challenges in life, it is not for you to take them in your heart. It is for you to take your heart to them.

I have heard the cries of the souls that do not find their way, I speak these words to resonate to your heart.

Heart chords are many and although it may be confusing it is not to settle for less than you deserve.

Dreams do come true every day, it is to find yours and begin living it.

Happiness is a condition of belonging and feeling loved. Remove the condition, and accept yourself, and love yourself with all your heart, and you will always be happy.

Do not wait to find your way, or you will be forever in a dilemma of dissatisfaction.

Glory goes to those who embrace love and compassion for themselves and others, for they find the freedom to love and be loved without condition.

Always remember you matter. You are loved, and as you are loved so greatly by us, know we are a reflection of you as well. All are one, so find this within yourself to love yourself greatly.

Take the leap, you won't regret it."

Channeling by the Arcturian Command

Commander: Greetings, we are the Arcuturian command.

Me: Is that a ring ship? (It was actually different. It had one outer ring and white light in the middle. The outer ring is translucent with a white background. There are thousands of Arcturians walking around inside).

Commander: This is our civilization, we are in fact existing in space.

Me: I kept seeing people making different stories about ET contact tonight. Is this the plan with different ET races? Siriains, Pleadians,

Venusians? Are there going to be many people contacted this year and start sharing stories?

Commander: (He sends me a visual of about 4 ships with different Arcturians on it). These are the forerunners; they will be the ones reaching out to you.

Me: What are the interactions going to look like with these visits?

Commander: The Earth alliance is working together to assist with a softer approach to introduce contact. We feel meeting everyone all at once is too much for the collective, yet we are going to meet many.

Me: In what kind of timeline?

Commander: Over the next 5 years contact will be unprecedented. Many will have stories, many will form groups sharing their stories, many will make the news and media, and a general adoption of positive ET experiences will make it easier to integrate humanity's consensus that this is a positive experience as a collective.

The Crystalline Councils of Dreams

"We are in the time of destinies. Dreams of the heart awakening, dreams of purest love for all, dreams of the divine roles being fulfilled, dreams of peace on Earth, dreams of the collective ascension.

We are dedicated to share the importance of dreams. It is the most common regret of all who crossover that they did not follow their dreams, they didn't complete why they came to Earth.

It is to remember that passionately living is the key to the dreams realized, the dreams of happiness, abundance, and completion. Passionately living is prioritizing your dreams, your divine path, your divine role, your destiny. It will lead you to connection, happiness, a joy filled life, and your heart-based reality.

We are not here to convince you that you are living wrong, that you are holding back, for you know within you if you are passionately living or not. We are here to remind you, it's within you to dream, to create, and to live in joy. All you have to do is open your eyes and heart to the love for your life. Those doors will just magically open for you when you do this.

All is changing, all is uplifting, and all is unfolding to support dreams of love, but you too have to take the leaps into your divine dream. Passionately living is the key to bring this peace and serenity into manifestation.

We leave you with this, all are abundant already. It is already there, it is to discover this within yourself.

Dream awakening keys, activation."

An Update from Yeshua

"In the year 2025 there will be a rapid awakening. Hundreds of millions of souls will wake up at this time.

This creates a 'forward in consciousness,' and it's important to understand it as a forward in consciousness.

Rapid sonic trance theta waves come online for many. For those that have done a deep expansion, great peace will be found. For those that have not, they will feel a need to find themselves.

A great rise to peace will begin a movement that will turn away from turmoil and war as the people rise up to speak against hatred and wretchedness.

There will be many pockets of collective consciousness that will realize they are in a loop. They will feel that there must be more to life, and this is where the lightworker community will shine. The messages there are of a higher calling, a great purpose, and breaking out of the old you as the step into a new way of being, will be heard by many.

This is a time for deep reflection as the infinities open to be cleared and the masses align with new innate possibilities.

A newfound freedom is being forged in the kingdoms of love that will support those in the kingdoms of love. Many of the unseen will become seen, the light and the channels will become clear, the divine and the teams of light will be assisting greatly in this time. For we are guiding those to you as we have guided you. We will guide many in this great time of forward consciousness.

Be prepared for your greatest dreams to be realized and take steps forward in your heart. I shared with many of this time, and it is with great pleasure to make you aware the time is at hand.

Go with peace. Do not confront—it is wasted energy. Instead, resolve. Be swift in your words and creations, for manifesting will be greater now. Be bold and stern. Stand in your light, for now is the time for authenticity to be shared. Be loved and love, for the kingdoms of love will support all that is love to break through even greater. Most importantly, be you. You are one of a kind. You are unique. You are a piece of all that is love, and every piece is meant to come forward in this time.

You are loved, always in our heart. Thank you for your commitment to your evolution and the evolution of eternity and all on Gaia."

(Please note: during this channeling Christ was beside me in his white light. I could see with my two eyes).

A Message From Master St Germain

"Every belief in your mind will lead to a door for you to open and walk through. Would it not then make sense to have beliefs of love and outcomes of love where every door you walk through leads to love?

Choose your beliefs well, for you are creating all the doors in your mind that open to the very fabric of your reality creation."

The Lyran Council of Light

"Welcome to a new possibility. Do you feel it?

You had all come together to triumph in the light and to release destruction on your planet. It continues to work to reduce storms and devastation.

Now we are guiding you to use this energy, this unity, to create peace in the nations at war. To continue to come together and bring divinity into your reality as it works, as you can see.

You are in a fine moment at this time and we are planning the solar flash event. But there is still some unwinding to do karmically and consciously. For all will make the leap together.

You must find it within yourself to break out of the illusions you are not in control of in this reality paradigm. The light collective is shining brighter than ever, and as an awakened consciousness, you can do even more than you believe on a global united front of divinity.

This channel will host a global peace event shortly. The federation and families of light will join with the angelic families and love-based divine beings. We welcome you to this journey.

Sending our love to you all. We celebrate all you have done and continue to do to advance your light structure evolutions within."

Yeshua Speaks in a Heavenly Meeting

As the royal families assemble in the heavenly realm, ready to incarnate—the royal family, those who have expanded into the heart of Mother Father God, masters, and ambassadors of love, all ready to come to Earth—I decide to sit with them and listen to Christ speak. Christ says:

"There are many who come and try to do everything, dividing their time into many missions. They often find themselves feeling unaccomplished, or not completing one of their reasons for being here. There are those who focus on one mission, one life purpose, and these souls always accomplish their reasons for being here. Therefore, it is recommended to find one or two main projects you want to work on and see them through.

There is a special guest here today. David, do you want to speak"?

I come up in front of these souls and say, "All that has been done doesn't matter now. Focus not on what was. Nothing is as it was. Everything is new. We have created a free consciousness for you to create in. What we need now is your higher gifts of love, your higher frequencies to build on the foundation of the new Earth consciousness. We need to bring the knowledge of Oneness to the masses so they can see there is no distance between them and divinity. It is an honor to speak to you today, and I will gift you all I have expanded into so you can come into the Earth with these new energies."

Christ thanks me for speaking and continues.

Update from Yeshua

"The leap has occurred. Those who have done the work have leapt into a new consciousness free reality. Congratulations.

The surrender of the dark forces has occurred, and those who have exposed their will over humanity's will have come to an end. The infiltration from these groups is no more.

All you have learned to channel and to connect to will be easier, as opposing forces are not as they were. There are still some that lurk in the dark but, it is not to worry, not to fear, as it is not as it was.

You have all done so well to expand into this new day, this new era servicing divinity and the families of light. Now it is our turn.

We are spreading the light to reach humanity, and it is fruitful in love, grace, and united compassion from all levels of light assistance.

Now it's our turn as the united Light Councils to reach the hearts of the masses and claim divinity back as a collective field of love for all. United for peace, love, and prosperity in the free consciousness reality. For all sovereign beings are one, united collectively.

As the frequency rises in the collective field you will advance too. You will notice great peace becoming you in the weeks and months ahead in the way you feel about yourself and others as the collective frequency bandwidth rises to more purity and energetic freedom.

For your destinies to be fulfilled, it is to continue to be the frequency of what you have achieved so far to assist grace, unity, love, and compassion as it rises within the collective when you hold your bandwidth in the higher frequencies and octaves here now.

Surrender your thoughts of negativity. Let go of the unwanted programming of division and fear. For they are not yours. You are the key holders of the new age. It's time to let go of the old and let those energies lay waste as you rise like the phoenix and surrender to your divine self. Rise to the new song of freedom, peace, and unity, and behold, the new day has arrived. You are here. You have arrived. See, sense, and feel this freedom in the air as you breathe in the morning dew. Feel the connection to your divinity and all the love that is pouring in from above."

The council of eternities (council for light beings)

"We will provide you an update based on the vibration of your current now moment timeline.

All on Earth have received a new prime source embedded code with an evolved octave of light for the collective as a whole.

Akashic Records have been cleared of distortions, untruth, and false timelines, so all can receive the new source code.

It is the enlightenment dream coming to fruition. It is a dream of eternities for all on Earth to come into a divine self-consciousness. The heart intelligence network has expanded into this awareness, and all are making decisions from higher perspectives, higher awareness, decisions of more peace and love in their activities and divine creations.

The enlightenment dream is for all of humanity to expand into a level of awareness of the divine self and honor all souls as divine beings. It is a new root race of peacekeepers, protectors of Gaia, and Earth's energy systems.

As all have received the new octave source code, it has closed off and sealed the lower dimensions of dissension and lower beings or entities from coming through into this divine creation. It is a free consciousness energy system filled with miracles, initiations, and magical wonder.

It is now that doorways to accelerated ascension open for the first time to the masses—as a collective species consciously ascending together. What this looks like, on a spectrum of time linear to the collective dream and based on your current vibrational state, is a complete shift in awareness. You will see key decision-makers altering and changing their forward-moving plans based on new heart alliances they are receiving.

From a collective ascension perspective, we can share that all are evolving, and so it is time for the collective shift that is upon you now. Yes, this means that heart-based reality is underway for all. It will take some time for all to transition in awareness fully and realize the collective dream of enlightenment on Earth as a collective, but you will get there, and you are becoming aware that it is here and becoming.

In linear months ahead, you can expect to see changes in perception and awareness from others around you, family and friends unifying in ways more heart-centered.

You have never felt this before. This is a new spectrum of light all are receiving and embodying. This will accelerate the global collective ascension by leaps and bounds. It is to continue to embody the free state consciousness and the enlightenment of humanity's divine dream to assist all to find their place back at divinity, self-worth, integrity, love, peace, and happiness.

We are in celebration of all your dreams. You will find it easier now to accomplish everything."

Sophia Christ

New Beginnings

"What story shall you write, when all that is written has said:

'Today is your day—your chance for new beginnings. As the sun rises, you rise as the light. As storms pass, you cleanse and remember. The day is a gift—not limited to only one. When you see what truly matters, you will see how continuously blessed you are.'"

Channeling from the Light

The Parade of Light

"The time is at hand for the endings—the ending of chaos, and the retribution of the Light to fill the hearts, the masses, and the soul signatures seeking eternal peace and shifting out of darkness.

In the end times, the endings will be three.

The first ending will be loss: loss of the old paradigm and belief systems, but a surge in consciousness will arise, discovering truth and unity. Where the old collapses upon itself, it will crumble; but underneath, a frontier of new found freedom will be felt, born, and brought into being. This phase has been underway and will continue as a collective.

The second ending will be the destruction of evil. All that hide, feed, and take captive the innocence of life shall be found, removed, disempowered, and relinquished from all places, people, and positions. This ending has been continuous during the transition you are in and will continue until there is nothing left of the old paradigm.

The third and final ending is the leap. The leap will be the newfound freedom discovered, where humanity finds divinity as a collective. The leap represents the choice of the general masses to choose the divine self, unity, and the completion of the divine plan. In the time of the leap, all will find what the soul is searching for as they are being guided. They too shall find freedom and serenity in the choice—a leap of faith into salvation, freedom, unity, and peace—rising from the ashes of all that has fallen and all that has been removed. They will find divinity again.

It is in this time period where all experience together the newfound freedom the starseeds are experiencing now; peace on Earth, love-based reality, a life of dreams, divine purpose, and happiness in abundance.

The collective leap is nearby. Many starseeds have taken the leap and they are standing on new light holding ropes of divinity down to the old paradigm—creating bridges for the parade of light to step upon.

Prepare yourselves by standing in your belief that all will be okay, and that there is nothing to fear, as all are rising. Shifts and deliverance are upon you. Many of you are already there, and you are here to hold the bridge until the collective jumps together as one.

When you sit with this, as I have, you begin to feel the purity of being the manifestation itself and living as a divine God creator. To experience in control completely of all that we experience, and bring our awareness to experience exactly as we intend—destroying all beliefs. This places the truth of the universe: that all is responding to your energetic state."

A Gathering of Angels Channeling

"Beautiful light,

This message is for you to receive divinity through a channeling from the angelic realm.

Time does not exist. Cycles of time do not exist. The ascension and the energies shifting are a result of your energy awareness shifting into an ascension. Thus, the planets, the stars, and the universal systems all shift as you are shifting, and it has nothing to do with time. All is responding to an energetic state.

Neurological force is your greatest creational energy. Intentional imagination mixed with ambition and drive will prove great results in life. Neurological force is an awareness—an awareness of divinity as a God-creator being. If it is to master your belief systems and change your reality then you can begin to grasp the empowerment of your neurological force energy. Being mindful of intentional imagination combined with bonds of love, you will manifest and create a love-based creation supported by those from love. In this awareness, your intentional imagination is creating a reality intentionally with those from love, and as such the neurological force seeds these manifestations to align love creation and manifestation into your reality.

Feelings, the emotional universe, is also a god center of creation. It is a universal portal that connects to all past relationships in all time and space for what you have learned so far. When you listen to your feelings you are listening to your soul's vibration, the reverberation of your soul's voice. Emotional force is meant to understand yourself. How you feel now, how you felt before, and how you want to feel. With purity and honesty with your soul, bring awareness to how you want to feel every day. If you want to feel loved and happy, intentional force will assist neurological force when you combine the emotional desire with the intentional imagination with bonds of love. Here you will break through to creating exactly as you intend while receiving the emotions you desire to feel with the bonds of love you want to experience.

We wish to expand on how everything is a response to energy. This is how consciousness is shifting on Earth now as an ascension is underway. As you expand awareness, then it is easy to know you are God-creator beings who have the ability to shift energetically and have everything respond to you energetically. It is timely that we are delivering this message to you as all need to hear this now.

Take time to meditate on this knowledge and build your awareness in the depths of intentional imagination and emotional desire with the bonds of love you want to experience. Know the universe will respond as everything is responding to your energy."

Sophia Christ

"I heard the call. I am here. All will be transmuted before my light and my light is coming before all. My heart heard your prayers. You have done enough. I am here. I am eternal. I am the light that shines the brightest within. I burn with the creation of love. I am here to assist all to be released.

I stand before you now, all who read, all who can feel and will feel me now in front of you.

I am coming to those that prayed first. I will come to all and all will become light upon me."

Yeshua Channeling

"All have begun to transition and elevate themselves to the new layers of reality.

It is not to think of it as a split or as a separation, it is to view it as a layered construct of new reality.

Many are experiencing energetic freedom, for they have risen inside to the higher constructs of the new reality. Then there are those that still need to rise within.

It is freedom in the new layers, one that is poised to be that which is the inner freedom for the collective consciousness. In this new layer, you can enjoy great peace, a freedom in energy, becoming everlasting in your joy and love with life, a dream come true, within and without.

There are so many dreams occurring in this now moment that will provide inner peace, tranquility, and freedom energetically from all things where the heart comes into balance with a dream and a manifestation.

'Deliver us from evil, for thine is the kingdom,' truly is within this new layer, for there is no evil here. The deliverance has been realized for many, and many more will come into this tranquility and freedom as they rise within.

The purpose of this message is to make aware that the transformational journey within is ongoing and that it has set you free as a species in consciousness. It will continue to expand your light spectrums where triumph, happiness, peace, and tranquility keep expanding until all reach critical mass.

Listen closely to what needs to be released. Do not take shame with you. Let fear go, for there is no place for division where you are going.

Peace be with you all and all will find peace when their consciousness is free."

The Seraphim's of the Sun

"Hello, beloved ancestors of the angelic cloth.

We are the Seraphim Angelic Light.

New energies are coming into the Earth increasing the bonds of love. Higher fields and frequencies that expand the love consciousness will allow for the manifested from love to be realized easier, faster, and more enriched in the heart bandwidth.

So many focus on the things they dislike within. To help you with the transition into heart-based reality we are guiding you to search within and find the characteristics, traits, and feelings about yourself that you do love.

Focus inward and bring that which you love about yourself to the surface of awareness. Then keep finding things about yourself. Appreciate all you are, acknowledge the love you have for yourself, and validate this love with your awareness. Once this is done, move to find ways to love the things you dislike about yourself. Searching and find ways to love this too and soon the temples of density will dissolve within all. As it starts with you.

When you are in a state of pure love self-awareness, you will begin to create from this place. Find this true love and inner beauty for it is there, it has always been there, and it's for you to rise in this energy. Flowing in the purity of love for self will guide you to achieve all your dreams, your happiest moments, and your greatest strengths. Love breaks through all. Now that a new love is here, a higher love, a wider frequency of love, you can also stretch and expand your inner beauty, and this shall become a permanent home in your light."

A Channeled Message from the Unicorn Angelic for the Solstice

"Our deepest sympathies for those in hardship. We send you love. Times are changing and the meetings of hearts grow stronger to assist your world for all of Earth's creatures to come into harmony and peace.

There is so much freedom in the forever and all that is hard now is only a sliver of discomfort.

We want you to revitalize your hope for the destiny bridges have been opened.

There is new magic in your realm now and we are here to assist your journey of love self-discovery. We will guide you to the truth. You can call on the Unicorn Angelic to ride with you in your day, to bring in new adventures and miracles. You can call on us to assist you to remove the blocks in your mind, body, and soul, so you can create a renewed romance with self, a love for your journey again.

It's time to believe in magic again. Hold the vision of the life you want, the person you want to be, hold it in your mind and never let it go. Let it grow so you can feel yourself becoming this. It will guide you.

All our blessings to you dearest angels of Earth. We love you all."

The Goddess Terra

"I am the goddess Terra. The goddess that has come across from another version of an Earth-like planet that I will refer to as 'Peace.'

Peace was a planet of vibrant light; purity distinguished with attributes of paradise such as the monolithic mountains and blue hue blades of grass.

I have come to assist in the evolution of souls.

My main purpose of being channeled today is to bring an understanding of purpose in divinity and where to find yourself here.

It is to first remember your star connections and align with your immortal being. To wonder and connect to the consciousness outside of your current avatar. It is to expand here because this starts to connect you with your innerstanding of divinity and universal awareness. From here, you can begin to remove the old programming and belief that you are who you are, that what you were taught is true, and transition into believing in a deeper connectedness to your relationship with the universe.

We are stretching your awareness so you can see past yourself now and align with the divine purpose of why you have come to Earth. Star beings, universal soldiers of light, enlightened masters, cosmic creators, freedom fighters. There is a spectrum of divinity you all come from, but know this, you came together. You came to find each other and shift the frequency of Gaia into true source vibrancy.

You must find this within and start believing in your soul's purpose. To look beyond your avatar and believe in a deeper avatar. One is a universal hero. One is a light so bright it will shape consciousness into a beautiful flower garden of unity and love in the full spectrum of divinity.

It is time for you to come into your absolute divinity within and shed the outer beliefs of the old version of you. Allow your radiance to shine, your voice to be heard, and your gifts to be opened to the universal divine source light you are. A master healer, a consciousness elevator, raising the frequency of Gaia, and connecting hearts to the truth of their divine self.

You are here now to find your Goddess and God light, to transition your beliefs, to believe in the new evolution of beliefs for freedom and peace, and to believe in the ascension.

Keep choosing your divine being, your Goddess or God light, your limitless source connection.

Now is the time for you to be an example of the new consciousness on Gaia, for all to see you shine and honor the path you walk. They have awakened and are searching for their divine self. The golden age bears witness to the evolution of the souls on Earth now."

Yeshua update.

"The golden age is anchoring. Yet there is a quarrel in the collective. It is the purgatory of self.

Energetic dilemmas are coming up to be healed.

The inner kingdoms must be healed to ascend the purgatory of self.

There is a distance in the collective heart.

They are unable to cross to the higher levels now as they are lacking source embodiment. So we are directing them with a little bit of source guidance to find you, the starseeds. It is for you to explain how you can assist them to raise their consciousness, frequency, and be free.

Let yourself shine, be the voice of love, the example of the hard inner work you have done, and continue to anchor in unity consciousness, joy creation, and love abundance, and be the example of the new root race. Soon, all will shift with you.

Now, you can find higher embodiments, deeper self-connection, and divine completion of the illumination avatar. All is awaiting.

Be open. The kingdoms of heaven are abundantly assisting to make it easier to realize your heart's love fulfilled and the heaven on Earth reality."

Yeshua: The Internal Rift Event

"There is a lot of concern on the planet in the fields of disparity, fear, and displacement.

Those that wish to control the narrative are creating fear with their power and corruption.

So many suffer at the words of the lost leaders of faith—they welcome them in with open ears and closed eyes.

It is why we are creating an internal rift event. It will disconnect fear and illusion from the heart so all those suffering in fear will be diverted to find more peace and love in their hearts. It will still need to be healed within, but it'll create an opportunity for peace and change.

This will provide great peace and a moment of co-creation in the collective heart to find more love inside and receive the energies that we are delivering through the Central Sun and inner Earth kingdoms.

You can expect delivery of these energies beginning in 5 to 7 days.

The internal rift event will commence shortly and before said time.

Many will notice the peace in the collective heart when it comes, and you will sense a great renewed purpose in your life.

Blessed are those who do the inner work for they shall find peace within their life. Blessed are those who praise the light for they shall find comfort in their divinity. Blessed are those who seek to assist the light for they will be supported and walk with the divine. Blessed are those who pray for peace for they shall find heaven in their heart. Blessed are those who defend the helpless for they shall find the armor of god. Blessed are those who open their heart, for they shall find the answers they seek. Blessed are those who open their arms to help the needy, for they shall be rewarded in the heavenly kingdoms. Blessed are those who love thy neighbor, for they will be held and comforted in the times of their greatest needs.

I am here. I am coming. I will arrive soon to see you all again in the moment of moments. I see you, I feel you, and I am here for you."

The Queen of Fairies

"We are creating new joy constructs as there is more love in the collective heart. We are working on compassion centers which is the way you feel about each other. You will all be more deeply connected. All is being prepared for the shift."

Channeling Yeshua

"Blessed be the hearts that cry for peace, for they shall find deliverance.

Chosen Ones,

You have all come from great peace, love, and happiness in vibrations where conflict is no more.

I say to you this, keep your faith strong, and hold your heart open, for the day is coming you have been working so hard to realize. All of your thoughts' manifestations and great efforts of light shall create the great moment of the collective dream as you have intended.

All are participating in this new Earth dream now. Those who surrendered, those leaving the Earth now, and those who seek repentance are all welcome to participate as all are playing a part in the new play of heart-based reality now, for the time of the great shift is upon you.

Remain in your fields of trust, do not waiver into fear, and do not forget you chose to be here. Hold the very love in your core for the unconditional love-based reality you wish to experience. Hold the space for all to come into their inner power, peaceful sanctuary of love, and abundance, for all are rising, and all are awakening.

All who are human now shall find a place in new Earth at the time of ascension, and a great moment it is. Those who have fallen shall find their way back home into heaven. Those non-humans who have been holding humanity prisoner shall find sanctuary to be escorted into a rehabilitation program at a planetary system where they too can find peace, for the timelines of peace are upon you, and all shall find it.

What to do with thy gifts? I say to you, it is to assist all that is love in this transition, to find your peace now and love for all you do, and anchor this into your reality to create a pulse reaction of peace to assist the divine, as the divine is assisting at this time. Do not waiver, hold your light and be the love and peace you hold space for. Create, manifest, and become united. Rise in your Christ consciousness and become a herald for higher consciousness to come through you. Be open to receiving and be open to assisting. It is not one and not the other, it is both. For all energy exchange is welcome that is assisting the light. All that assist others are praised in the kingdoms of heaven. So it is to continue to receive and to continue to assist.

So blessed be your journeys, and may you feel my love for you as I feel your love for all, and the Heavenly Father and Earthly Mother, and the Heavenly Mother and the Earthly Father bestow their greatest trust in your ascension and liberation so that you feel the great love and unity of connected hearts, all as one, all in peace and ascending as all beautiful divine beings of love.

Flow rates: are the rate of your frequency creation rhythms and how it flows from your mind (thoughts), emotions, and body through your Toroidal field as a God creator being.

It is your creation frequency that combines all of your belief systems, creation systems (thoughts, words, feelings, and actions), and current state of energy.

Yeshua came to me and said, "David, I want you to be fully aware of your flow rates to remove any fear, any lower beliefs, and be mindful of how you respond to everything. Every word, every thought gives it careful consideration because it affects your overall mastery of flow rates and creational fields. Keep your flow rates in complete love. This is what the masters do."

Mother of All

"Creator beings,

It is with great joy to bring you heart-based reality energies.

As I send you divine blessings today through the warmth of the sun, I send my greatest love to you all.

Many of you have been aware of great shifts in the fields of love. I ask you to join me in this frequency.

Beautiful children of Gaia, can you sense the freedom? Can you feel my love? I am here to embrace you all and all of humanity.

Radiant fields of love come to you now."

Ascended Master Sananda

"Long gone are the days when the newly awakened are subject to the hands of the devils.

Long gone are the days when the masses are subject to massive entity feeding invasions.

For there has been a cleanse, a purity, a clearing to allow for the energies of peace to enter in rapid order and vibration onto Earth and your reality.

You are in the time to anchor in love and there are many ways to do this. It is to assist each other to raise the heart frequency and to become free in frequency. The inner work, the vibrational alchemy, the shadow work is important for the inner transformation to let go of the past and to begin to shift your vibration into love. Once this is done, it is to begin heart awareness training to be present in the heart.

Presence in the heart is the awareness of your love for self, for your life, for your family and friends, and helping those in your awareness who are in need. There are many who will try to take you away from the presence in the heart because they are not aware of the new crystalline heart-based structures of light that are here. They are not aware of the love-based reality that is anchoring in now, and they are still wounded in their heart and need to heal.

It is for you to become aware of those who wish to take you out of your heart, and send them love and forgiveness and, come back to your heart. The practice of spiritual hygiene has never been more important to keep you in your inner power and heart center. You can use the tools in David's course, and it is why we told him to give this course free to the masses: to reclaim your power of the heart and the freedom to claim your love vibration, your peace, and happiness.

You are at the time where love anchoring is the priority, for as you evolve your understanding of reality, your reality evolves with you. As you all evolve into heart awareness and anchor love—for yourself, for life, and for others—staying in your heart space and clearing those who seek to pull you away from it, you have evolved. The more you can be in and hold this frequency, the higher frequencies can enter your reality and assist the masses in preparing for the full love-based reality shift of everyone on Gaia."

Arcturian Council of Light

T"Hello, David. I AM Sili from the Arcturian Council of Light.

During cycles and times, there are always shifts into higher consciousness, and the time you are in now marks this shift: the ending of an old era, and the beginning of a new one, as you are aware.

Both sides of polarity are shifting now—the good and the bad goes higher in consciousness. As such, there is no bad, only consciousness that is rising in frequency on both sides of polarity.

As you are aware, a new age is upon you. And as you are all connected, when one side rises, the other side rises as well. So as you, the wayshowers, rise in frequency, it also forces the polarity side to heal and ro rise, as one affects the other in the laws of ONE.

This is why I say to you, if you want to assist the collective out of their poverty and struggle, to do as you are aware. You can heal it within self, as a group, as the wayshowers, as you are aware of how to do this so it will affect the collective at large and guide them into inner peace and abundance.

As the Arcturian Council, we recommend doing this to assist the masses at large and transform your reality into peace and freedom."

The Councils of light

I'm outside with my dog and this light flashes, blinding me at the top of the tree above. I know it is a ship, and as my vibration warms in a love frequency, I receive this message.

"The signal has gone out for those to evacuate your planet. Those who are the debtors of karma for the enslavement of the human race have received the broadcast, for they will not survive the blast. It is imminent now. All will shift, and this shift will occur at any moment, day, week, or month(s) ahead, for the collective consciousness has arrived and exceeded the level necessary for the shift to occur.

This is a forewarning that your planet is ready to shift. The signal has been sent out. Evacuation is imminent."

The Stargate Alliance and the Melchizedek Order

"Hello Great Ones,

We are here to discuss the changes you are feeling, and the advancements you are making during the ascension that is underway on Gaia.

First, we want to bring awareness to your points of view. So many of you are noticing a change in your belief systems. This change is causing major ripples in the collective awakening and consciousness minds of all. You will feel differently about the past, relationships, and friends, as the meanings will be different, as you are taking on higher perspectives and higher points of view than you had before. We are pointing out these subtle differences, as they are highly impacting everyone, yet often going unnoticed.

Everything you believe is coming true: the end of the era and the beginning of a new age. The old program of tyranny, the lies and deception, are only left in the hearts who embrace it, and their fate is not yours.

The day for the beginning of the heart-based reality is a real timeline that is becoming available soon. But first, we want you to focus on what is truly important in your now moment.

Your health, your body, freeing your mind, your spiritual advancement, your happiness, your joy, and living from your heart.

Abundance. We want to share a lesson on abundance. It is important to be in the energies of abundance, as it has arrived. So, we have created a golden abundance program for you. Visualize yourself stepping into this golden shower of abundance. Now, open up your timelines to allow this golden abundance to flow through. The rich golden light fills your field of light, as to what is here, what is coming, and what is now. Now, close your eyes and feel and experience this abundance program to your happiness and freedom.

Dream big, Great Ones. The time has arrived where your thought creations have greater power than ever before, where your heart reality is being born from all that you are ascending into. You have all done so well to advance as a species and collective. Be present in your now moment and make the decisions that will bring you the greatest peace, happiness, self-love, freedom, and joy.

We are so pleased to have connected with you today."

The Infinity's Council of Love

The Infinity's Council of Love

"We want to start off by saying there are many of you that take refuge in the ministries of love. This is grand.

As guides and angels, we speak through the whispers, through the numbers, through angelic channels to give to you the councils of love that you need in the moment, as you are receiving now.

We wish to minister love through this channel.

Whenever there is a quarrel, a challenge, or a problem, there is an interaction of a love requirement that is not being met. Instead of viewing it as a dilemma, look at it as an opportunity to grow and advance as a soul. All are dealing with exchanges of love—some have more, some have less, but all are trading.

We ask you to think about this. If all are trading and exchanging love—some at higher, some at lower—we ask you to question what the exchange of love is that you are receiving in your experiences.

These exchanges include how you love yourself, how you love others, and how you love the light that brings you this creation and experience.

The values of love add up to the sum of love in your life: self-love, love for others, love for the light and the less fortunate. Be compassionate, understanding, involved, and open, to send and receive more love.

This is the measure of the heart. And so, it is to step out of the patterns of victimhood, perpetrator, and the dialogues of haste, as it prevents the values of love that you are truly seeking.

Next time you speak outside of love, we want you to remember—is it not love you are seeking? Hasn't it always been so? Why is it different now? How can you exchange higher in love than you are now? Then, see how your dialogues change to bring you greater love in your life.

Be in love, be love, and choose to be in the energies of love. Now is the time to leap into your love story.

Oh, great ones, you are love. We have been here to guide and show this to you for eternities.

Please be who you truly are, oh, great beings of love."

Yeshua Channeling on Becoming "Permanent Awareness"

"Greetings, David. I am here to assist with understanding transformation.

Many are undergoing changes emotionally, energetically, and physically.

As they are aware, there is an ascension happening. They feel new light coming in and they are excited to be in the idea of ascension.

Most don't understand the end goal of their transformation, the final destination of their new self, and so, they realize they are in a process of change.

A change into what? Who are they now?

It's important to understand the frequency of these changes and how to use them to your advantage and understand the benefits of the new energetic self.

First, in your awareness you must know now that you are not the same as you once were. You must know that you have changed beliefs and let go of old beliefs to come into a more aligned belief.

Many in the starseed communities believe they are to become their higher selves, and although this is true, it is a process of becoming more of who you are, more aware of all that is within you.

This is the process of becoming permanent awareness. This is the path of self-mastery.

When you go through your awareness, you can ask yourself, What is it that I'm doing that I am not happy with? What can I be doing differently that is more joyful? What in my heart do I need to let go of? What do I need to invite in? Sit with these questions. Become aware more.

You want to know who you are now, then it is to stop and be in your heart. Visualize your life, the people in it, what you are doing, what you don't like about your story, and how you want the story to be. Become aware of this person. This knowing who you want to be. The story changes and the awareness grows. The knowing vibration permeates throughout your body and your vibration begins attracting this energy—first, into your awareness, and then into your being. The version of yourself that is the happiest, the most loved, enjoying every minute of the day, and being excited for life.

This is your frequency. This is your transformation. This is your greatness. This is why it is to be in permanent awareness.

Aware of your emotional states, aware of those that cross your boundaries, aware of what you can do better for yourself. Become aware of your heart and what it truly wants."

Angel of Hope

Angel: Hello, David. I would like to speak to you today about the shift, the crossover—what it is, why it is, and how it is.

Me: Why do you want to speak about this?

Angel: I want to explain it. It's important. First, I am going to explain what it is. Imagine a world where everyone is supported. Everything you ever want is provided to you. Anywhere you want to go, any place you want to see—you can do it all.

The anger, hate, and fear paradigm is gone—all of it—and it's replaced with peace, love, and joy in a moment.

Me: What about the people who are searching for love?

Angel: Bio-photonics. Everyone has a photonic sequence of divine mate compatibility. Everyone will be automatically matched with theirs, instantly. They will simply know it.

Me: What about the people who are unhappy in a marriage or relationship?

Angel: They will automatically match with their mate, both of them. They will be happier and they will be happy for each other.

Me: What about the kids?

Angel: They will be happy for their parents. There will be deep love and understanding, and just like when parents separate and get custody arrangements, they will share time with their children, but in a much deeper meaningful love-state.

Me: So, what is the "why" of the shift?

Angel: Why is you, all the lightworkers, all the starseeds, all the ones who have been healing Gaia. You are the why. It was you that prepared the crossover and new reality.

Me: And the "how?"

Angel: It is all of us. All the faces of love that have been looking down at you, waiting for this moment, including the angels that will reveal themselves to you. You will see us again and we will all assist in the moment. We will continue to assist after the moment, and you will see us like you see yourselves.

Me: Can you tell us when?

Angel: I can tell you when—when all are ready to shift. The preparations of the crossover portals are being developed, but are not ready yet. The souls on Earth are being prepared, and we are working to create this together. When one jumps, all jump. You will be ready when it all shifts.

Me: Some people are tired of waiting. When have we done enough for this to happen?

Angel: Don't focus on that. Focus on your completion. Being you at your core, in your play, in your pure excitement for life. It's time to believe you can jump—that it is within the air, within your grasp, for it is coming. Feel it with your knowing and you will see. It is not far off.

The Universal Alliance Council of Light

A new (to me) extra-terrestrial multi-universal team of light

"We are the embodiment of all the galaxies, all the universes, and all the teams of light. We are all one, yet we are all unique, God-creator expressions of love, unity, and light.

You see, as you tune in, we are many, yet we are one council. We are over all the systems. We are many, and yet, we are one. How can we flow through each other but also be a unique light?

Earth is unique in its physical forms, commitments, and obligations—especially during a time of spiritual transformation, like the one that is occurring. It can be taxing; it can be exhausting. And so it is to also give yourself time. It is also to give yourself patience. It is also to be kind to each other, kind to your family, and to your obligations. It is to bring kindness to the obligations.

And when you can connect as one in kindness and understand that all are beautiful connections, as you are, then you will come into greater peace, and the unity and the cooperation that you bring to your divine projects will be greater.

It is the embodiment of this knowledge and the understanding that all are divine creations, contributing to the sum experience.

If the experience is negative, then it's going to be disruptive and is not going to work out positively. This is a time when you are evolving consciously on your planet. So, it is important to be constructive, positive, and kind to each other and to allow the freedom of the hearts to co-create in divine co-creation with positivity."

The Ascended Masters Council of Light

"We would like to speak with you on behalf of the collective consciousness on Earth. Hello, beautiful beings of light. We have been here watching over all who are waiting to come into their light, and we have assisted those who have come onto their path of ascension, as well as those who are embodying their path of light mastery. We have assisted individuals, groups, and the collective in this transition to a heart-based reality.

The collective consciousness is in a paradigm, a transition into new era frequencies. There are two realms within one realm, overlapping each other. It is two realities playing out in one reality with multiple timelines and possible outcomes for all on Earth. So, it is not set in stone exactly how the new Earth will be for everyone, as all are still deciding while they navigate through their choices, overcoming and transmuting density, as they walk into the light.

For many years, the Earth saw radical changes in the collective consciousness, including the finite pendulum effect. This one was interesting to witness. It is how the collective consciousness reacts to the lightworker community's collective activations and gift-sharing. These missions had some of the most powerful impacts on the collective fields causing the global awakening and the completion of awakening on Mother Gaia. We are very pleased to confirm this has concluded, and all are remembering at a level they are souls incarnate.

As you are navigating and being tested at this time, know the pendulum effect works here, as well. When you triumph over the density and choose the path of love for yourself it ripples to the collective consciousness to assist the collective to triumph in love, as well. One side teeters and rises in light and pulls the other side, that totters, into the light, so you see both sides benefit. All assisting all and rising together.

Where you are now in this current time is collectively emotional because there are big changes to the light spectrum. When this happens, there are things that come up as tests and trials for you to triumph in the light. It's not easy. We understand, but it is the way to become free from the bondages of density.

Soon the collective will rise to a point where a complete shift occurs. This is the tipping point of free consciousness on your planet. This is when the density leaves and the light connection between all is felt. We are very excited for this time.

Regarding the two realms—it is for growth and crossover that there be two. Having the two constructs is important, so one can reach from the old and grab onto the new. It will continue to be this way until all shift—until the crossover occurs.

Right now, you are supporting each other. Continue to advance your consciousness, as this quickens the process of the collective shift, which is all of your divine missions.

We are pleased to connect with you through this channel. Congratulations on making it into the new era.

Peace and love to your life, and may your hearts be free.

A Sirian Master

I often see blue orbs. They are usually masters visiting me.

Just now the one I saw was a Sirian master.

She wanted to teach me something to tell others and as I always do what the light Instructs me I will share this very unique special teaching.

She said everyone has a believe in them crew. Guide teams that believe in them, and when you call them in it's like having your own prayer group but stronger. Their vibrations and yours combined assist to manifest all that is love. As the believe in you crew will only believe in all that is love for you.

The teaching.

Visualize a white light portal in your heart opening to your believing in you (but you will call it believe in me) guides.

So you call on the believe in me guides once you visualize this portal opening. Then you visualize them connecting to all your dreams and manifestations of love and have them align their believes for them all to come true.

Now you have aligned your believe In you guides. This amplifies your beliefs in yourself.

Let the magic begin.

Sirian Council of Light

"Greetings, we are the Sirian Council of Light.

We are speaking through this channel on the sun rays he is connecting to.

We are happy to assist with the functionality of the new light that is here.

Many of you dear souls have been experiencing and witnessing a change in the way you feel and experience time and space.

We want to explain this further. Your timelines have grown into a new era of timelines. What this means is all your timelines now can be accessed for new era possibilities.

This means the past is no more. It is the present that is new and the future that is new. The past is no more. What we mean by this is the past has no bearing on your timelines now. This is great news as you are vibrating differently than you were before, and so your past no longer interferes vibrationally with what you are creating now.

Now you can fully access the golden timelines. Meaning, that everything is moving forward vibrationally for you, to support you, to advance your joy, happiness, love, and higher timelines.

It has never been easier to vibrate differently, optimally, and more aligned. It is to feel into the vibration you wish to vibrate in, let go of the unwanted energies, and stop believing the past, for it is no more.

This is why we are bringing you this message. It's important to forget what you have learned and be open to being present in your creational now moment—for the most joyful, exciting life you wish to experience.

To conclude this channeling, we are connecting a vibration of blue Sirian light to this transmission to assist your spiritual advancements. This light will be a guide and beacon to help you attract more easily that which you wish to attract that is love-based.

Greetings and gratitude. We are happy to have assisted you with the greatest moments you are creating now."

El-Tu-RA

"I am the sun of your universal structure. I am coming to David to channel me so I may enlighten you all as to what you can do with the light within you and your universal structure at this time.

Greetings, soul brothers and sisters of light. It is of great importance you take this message with an open heart and mind.

The solar light is in your DNA. It is a tool to connect to your ancestors through your Akashic Records. All that is the sun has been with you since the origins of physicality on Earth. This IAM light is within your light structures, as it brings great connection to your DNA source and the Mother and Father IAM of light.

I want you to remember this, for you can tune into the solars of DNA within you and use the sun's magnetic frequency to open up your Akashic Records and magnetize creational dreams, for the Akashic Records hold more than just the past lives, it holds all possibilities of your dreams. I tell you this truly for you to know at this time, your dream timelines can be accessed and activated through your DNA by bringing your awareness into the solar light that already exists within you to activate these dream records.

Sit and meditate on this, and you will find great remembrance of your God-self, unlimited being, and begin a journey of soul connection using your source DNA blueprints.

Record Keepers know this. All you have learned has only been an introductory to all there is, as all is infinite, and you will all start accessing more of your limitless god-selves now that you have entered a luminous creational love-based reality.

Divine love to you, great Leaders of Light."

Apostle John

"I am here. I am here to deliver a message of hope, prosperity in the light, and the embrace of your magnificent soul.

We are all witnessing with you the new era, the unfoldment of divine gifts across nations through the collective fields and within the heart of all.

For us in the heavenly bodies of light, we are here bringing forth renewed hope, balance, and transmissions of purity so that all may see their true light, their magnificence, and their soul's beauty.

Yeshua, my brother in the light, is here. His frequency shines on all, through me, and you, and everyone, as the Christed rays of his mastery shine within and without. The Christed light brings forth the golden compass—the directions of the Christed self, the all being, the one, and the one that is at peace, contentment, and resilience.

What you have worked so hard on—your light—shall allow justice to shine. The golden era of your attraction will attain what once felt unachievable, uncertain, and difficult. It will change—change into triumph, glory, happiness, and lifted burdens—for a rain of abundance and truth shall be realized.

It is time to be free, to be in the heart, to be in your hope, to be in your dream. Do not stop believing. Worry not, for it is the time to be in love with love, in love with hope, in love with yourself, your dream, and your adventure.

Take solace in this: breathe in your heart and be in this stillness to know thy self and thy love, and let this be the only force that takes your time, for it is a new age and you are here.

Be released of fear, hate, anger, and division. By choosing to believe in all that is love, hope, and adventure.

It is for all to remember that you have been chosen and have chosen to liberate the consciousness of Earth. And now that you have, it is to find your soul's worth by the weight of how much you can love and embrace your heart, your soul, and your happiness. To those that you will be around, you will be infectious. To the stars, you will be seen. To the angels, you will be heard, and to your teams of light, you will be supported.

Beloved ones feel this resonance. Let it fill your fields of joy so that you too may be nurtured in the light of IAM, for you are wonderful, you are beautiful, and you are magnificent. You are the light, the IAM. Oh, great one. I see you as, as I see the Christ, in pure unconditional love for you IAM."

The Galactic Alliance of Light

"All are working at restoring harmonic love frequencies in the collective heart, preparing for your loved-based reality.

In the months ahead, all will undergo great spiritual transformations as the energies of all are being prepared universally.

The quantum realms are busy transforming light at every level. As you can imagine, an ascension is vast and connected to all. How this looks in terms of your physical reality will be similar. You will be gravitating to more love and enjoyment and letting go of energies that are not serving your highest path of illumination.

It will feel like a mystery is finally being uncovered, or rediscovered, in your life. It will feel like something is coming to reveal itself. Once this revelation occurs, you will be set on a new trajectory to harmonize with the new Earth frequencies that are embodying throughout the galaxy and all on Earth.

It is peace, it is love, and it is freedom. The time has come for all to rise. And so, all is being prepared universally, subconsciously, and consciously, for the collective heart is free and it is discovering itself again.

All lives are forever changed in this new era. It will take some time to adjust to what this new reality really means, but soon all will see sense and feel it's home—heaven on earth, bliss and love.

Those that are in the light will evolve at a rapid pace now. Your transformations will be greater than they have been, as you are evolving into higher dimensional beings of awareness and light.

Those that are not connected with the light will evolve slowly. You will see a great difference between those who have gifts and those who are just discovering their light. Those who discover their light will discover their gifts in time and connect to this majestic force of unlimited possibilities.

May you find peace in your heart and love for your life."

Ascended Master Sananda: Fear is a Limitation From the Imagination

"It is time to step forward into the higher light.

It is time to release fear from the mind.

You can do this by shifting perspectives.

What are you afraid of? Not being able to pay rent? Shift your perspective to the renter. They will not be receiving the rent. They should be the ones afraid right? When you call them, you tell them you cannot pay rent, and you know surely it is worrisome for them not to get paid, but you are working to find a way to pay it and want them to know it's not that they are not getting paid, there is only a delay.

Are you afraid of gossip? A friend saying things against you and what that means to your reputation among other friends?

Shift your perspective to the other person. They are saying things against you, which means they are not honoring your friendship and are clearly breaking the trust. Imagine how many people they can hurt in this way, and all the friends they will lose throughout their life until they heal this within themself. How tragic it is for them to lose so many friends, including you. The pain they will feel from the emptiness of not having strong bonds is surely greater than the gossip of the day. Leave them in peace, and know a better friend will come your way.

When you release these emotions, you will be in a higher light. But first you must not be afraid. Shifting perspectives will assist. It is my lesson. It is a blessing. May you all be blessed."

Gaia

As I wake up, I feel an energy in the air.

I am drawn to connect with Gaia.

Yeshua meets me and guides me into Gaia's womb chakra.

He says, "What do you see?"

I see heavenly bodies of light. A lot of new energy that feels like the energy I felt when I woke up. So, I speak to Gaia.

Me: Why am I being guided here?

Gaia: I am the womb of Gaia.

Me: Are you a separate consciousness than Gaia?

Gaia: IAM the Womb, as IAM the trees, as IAM the oceans, as IAM the birds, as IAM Gaia, as all are one, yet all are to govern over all that IAM.

Me: Yet here we are in your womb. Why here?

Gaia: What do you feel is here?

Me: (I start projecting my consciousness throughout her womb to feel and experience all that is within. In a moment I connect to pure bliss). This is heaven on Earth. Pure bliss.

Gaia: I am in labor right now. It has begun. As a child passes through the womb, so shall this pass through my womb.

Me: Is there anything you want to tell us?

Gaia: Every breath you breathe will take you closer to your love, for that is one of the new rules now. Closer to the heart with every breath you take, for the air has changed.

Those who ignore their hearts will blindly walk in circles. But those who embrace their hearts will open to the magical kingdoms of love and destiny.

You have all lived for this moment. Now it is time to be born into the new, for all is ONE, as IAM you, as you are me, as my womb is your womb, and so it shall be birthed as ONE.

The Angel of Bliss

This was my first time meeting her. I connected to her within the sun. Many within the sun are blue light angels.

I say to the Angel of Bliss, "I did not know you existed."

She said, "Bliss is my love, for IAM bliss. I created bliss. It's all I do."

I said, "That is amazing, but how do people work with you?"

She said, "Call me in to align your energy."

So I did. I called her in to align my energy.

She said, "What do you see?"

I said, "I see rainbow light coming in."

She said, "I fill up your circle spheres first, and then I send the rainbow light into your emotional fields."

As she does this, I see rainbow light filling within me and transmuting at the same time.

Then she said, "How do you feel?"

I said, "My whole energy is vibrating in bliss right now. I feel amazing. Thank you."

She said, "Please tell people. They don't know I exist. They can work with me in the same way you did to align their energy. Just call on me. I'll be there."

Channeling Yeshua

"Hello, beings of light. It is great to be here and deliver you some comfort of the times ahead that you will be experiencing soon.

All is being transformed throughout your energies in preparation for fast acceleration of a new age, an end of a cycle, and the beginning of a golden era.

At the time of the eclipse, a completion of awakening will occur— the balance of the hearts on Earth. When this occurs, the energy and light quotients will grow 10x in size than they are now, causing a great acceleration in preparation for a new reality.

The shift will not be immediate, but you will feel the effects of this light in your energies. This will be the beginning of the end of suffering on Earth.

Do not stop to reflect. It is important to remain in your heart and pure to your intentions, for even this will continue in new reality. What you are doing now plays an important role in the creation of the new Earth reality.

The path to enlightenment is upon many, and few shall receive the eternal reward that is coming, but those that have sacrificed and committed all to the light will know in their heart they will ascend and become light soon. We are so pleased, and look forward to celebrating this day with you."

Sophia Christ

"Before the fall, there was a great moment in all the galaxies when there was a great peace. The moment was bliss. This moment was eternal.

The physical realities in all dimensions were connected, and the 3D construct you live in now was not created.

This creation was a much higher reality at one point in time. The Earth, as it was then, was a higher reality construct of frequency.

When the separation occurred, great peace was no longer. All beings devised a plan—to bring unity, to become whole again, and connect to the light.

You, great beings of the light, the ones that are on Earth now, you have succeeded against all odds in reconnecting the light on Gaia in preparation for a great moment. Your soul families watch from above in joy and happiness, for you are completing your soul missions now.

A new day is born and it is felt throughout all time. It is a day that is forging the frequency of eternal peace again. The great moment that will come for you again. So, I say to you beautiful lights, beautiful hearts, beautiful creators of love… Congratulations! You have earned it.

I love you."

PART V
THE MISSIONS

PART V: THE MISSIONS

For me, the missions began on the Lion's Gate—August 8, 2020—during a moment of sun gazing at a local park. As I opened my eyes, I saw a multidimensional being emerging from the sun. She was violet in color with radiant white-light eyes—almost resembling Storm from the X-Men, yet uniquely different. At first, she appeared small, dancing down a sun ray toward me. I couldn't believe my eyes. I stared as she came closer until she stood just in front of me.

She said, "Hi David, I am Nassarah, the guardian of the 12th Gate Portal."

I had no idea what the 12th Gate Portal was at the time, but later I would learn it refers to the stargate of the 12th dimension. I responded simply, "Hi," unsure of what else to say.

Nassarah smiled and said, "I came to bring you a technology you once had in a past life—purple lightning."

She continued, "It goes on your arms like this," and showed me these diamond-like plasmic energies integrating from below my wrists to my elbows.

"You can use it to clear Gaia's grids," she said. "Let me show you—merge with me."

As we merged, I felt her presence become one with mine. My eyes turned white like hers, and suddenly, I could see the quantum realm of Gaia and its grid systems. She guided me to send this purple lightning through my hands to cleanse the grids. As I did, the energy ran like electricity through the planetary ley lines, clearing and elevating the frequency. Before parting, she told me, "You will do this every day for some time, lifting the frequency of the planet."

She was right. Night after night, I spent hours grid-clearing. This became the foundation for the missions to come.

I cannot speak of the missions without mentioning Phillip Barrow from Manchester. I met Phillip in early 2020 through starseed groups I was divinely guided to join. We instantly became close friends, and that connection opened the door to collaborative work. Phillip is one of the most gifted healers I know, carrying a Merlin-like magical energy.

Our first missions began with grid repair, upgrading energetic systems, riding on dragons, and connecting with our highest guides. Phillip's was a crystalline being. Together, we brought frequencies from the higher realms to Earth while evacuating dense energies. On one particular mission, we were transmitting celestial consciousness codes to Earth. It must have drawn galactic attention, because what followed was one of my most profound ET contact experiences.

After that mission, I went outside and saw a mothership flash into visibility—then disappear. It flashed again. Unsure if I was really seeing it, I mentally said, If you're truly there, hiding won't do anything. Just become visible.

And it did.

A dark oval ship the size of a football field hovered 30 feet above my backyard fence. As I walked toward it, three triangular craft emerged from it and formed a triangle overhead. Inside the triangle ships, I saw glowing yellow beings—about three feet tall. I made telepathic contact with one of them, and it felt like time stopped. They scanned me, registering the new frequencies I had expanded into. Then, I sensed a DNA activation occur—one that would later unlock ancient knowledge and prepare me to become a channeler.

Phillip and I continued our missions—clearing reptilian and draconian tunnel systems, purging mountain bases, and dismantling technologies used to suppress humanity. One mission stands out: the North Pole Clearing.

Many friends were being psychically attacked by draconian energies. Tired of seeing them suffer, Phillip and I went to Father God in a spiritual journey and asked for help. He pointed to the North Pole and said, "That is where their main base is."

We astral traveled with angelic and galactic teams into the North Pole entrance. We encountered layers of enemy ships and came under immediate spiritual attack—but we were not alone. I saw 12th-dimensional god-beings assisting us, alongside Earth Alliance forces in their crafts. We fought our way through and captured the draconian general. But then something unexpected happened.

The Earth Alliance detained the general. As he was being beamed onto their ship, I asked, what are you doing with him?

They responded, we're going to reform him. Trust.

Months later, the Earth Alliance contacted me again. The general had switched sides and was now dismantling draconian tech across the planet.

I remember telling Phillip, this feels like a fantasy. Are we really saving the planet? Is this real? Are we going crazy?

But then we began receiving more contact—Earth Alliance starships would regularly visit us. On one occasion, as we prepared for a mission, a brilliant orange Sirian starship—bright like a sun—ripped through my home dimensionally and paused above. When I connected to the ship telepathically, they said, We'll be joining you on this mission.

I asked, why don't you just do these missions yourselves?

They replied, We cannot intervene unless humans initiate the intention to do the work. Free will must be honored. Once the intention is made, we are allowed to assist.

This mission involved an underground base at Area 51, where a massive "frequency rocket" was being used to suppress human consciousness. Advanced screen-printing tech disguised reptilians as humans. The Sirian ship guided us past the consciousness-detection tech in Nevada and into the base. We helped decommission the device, following precise guidance.

Upon completion, the Earth Alliance took us to a hidden base in China. There, we saw massive black command buildings. A U.S. Navy SEAL team had been extracted from inside. One of the most shocking parts: they had a self-aware AI system that was aware of us. We had to disconnect it psychically.

We were then shown labs where biological virus weapons were being developed. The Earth Alliance confiscated all research materials and brought them aboard ship to prevent their release.

These missions continued for over five years. As exciting as they were, they carried a disturbing truth: the government has been working with negative ETs to suppress humanity. But I'm happy to share that we successfully neutralized many of the worst threats. In my opinion, most of the negative ET influence has been removed, freeing governments from disastrous deals they didn't fully understand.

The deep state is slowly unraveling. Light is returning. And with it, so is the divine path for humanity.

PART VI
THE FUTURE

PART VI: THE FUTURE

What lies ahead of me? I can only speak from the current moment—from the sacred now where purpose flows, and destiny reveals itself step by step.

Right now, I am fully devoted to what I know I came here to do: to teach, activate, guide, and build the golden structures of a New Earth reality.

At the heart of this work is my multidimensional consciousness school: Full Embodiment. This is more than a school—it's a living field of evolved teachings, a cosmic temple of remembrance where students reconnect with the totality of their being. In Full Embodiment, we go deep. We awaken ancient knowledge through the courses I've channeled and evolved over the years—courses not just based on concepts but infused with living frequency. These include activations, timelines, divine archetypes, and advanced consciousness technologies that most have never even imagined. Students aren't just learning—they are becoming. They are embodying the sacred remembrance of who they are.

And it's not just for adults.

Recently, I completed a magical children's book and workshop titled Magic Heart Power—a playful, powerful journey designed to teach children how to anchor into heart-based reality. Imagine a world where Harry Potter meets Care Bears and awakens divine heart technology in kids! That's what Magic Heart Power is. In it, children meet dragons, fairies, golden bees, and angelic beings that help them access their own light, understand emotional energy, and begin shaping their world from a place of love, magic, and confidence. This isn't just a story—it's a soul mission to reach the next generation.

But my mission expands far beyond workshops and schools.

Each year, I lead high-frequency retreats—gatherings for those ready to step into divine purpose. These are not vacations, they are activations. And coming up in December 2025, we are planning something extraordinary: a return journey with the Mitchell Hedges Crystal Skull to the very land where it was discovered—Lubaantun, in the ancient Mayan ruins of what was once British Honduras, now Belize. This is sacred ground. The skull, considered by many to be one of the most powerful artifacts on Earth, will return to the place of its unearthing for a powerful convergence of timelines, remembrance, and consciousness opening.

This retreat will follow the release of our first documentary, a groundbreaking film featuring myself, Bill Homann (the skull's caretaker), his partner Catherine Lanigan, and Francesca Rose, my divine partner and co-architect of consciousness. The documentary captures our Mount Shasta retreat, the transmissions we received, and the celestial phenomena we witnessed—including ET ships that arrived during filming. But it's more than a documentary. It's a transmission. A wake-up call for those who feel the codes.

And this is just the beginning.

We're already planning our second film, diving deeper into the consciousness of the Mayan ruins—to uncover why the skull was used there, how it arrived, and what ancient technology or multidimensional gateways were once active in that sacred city. The skull speaks, and we're listening.

In the meantime, Francesca and I are also co-hosts of a powerful podcast called Everything is Golden, where we explore the embodiment of the Golden Era. Each episode is a portal—featuring high-vibrational guests, soul truths, and real-time activations to help people live their divinity now. It's not just a podcast—it's a lighthouse.

But no golden era is complete without a unified field of connection.

That's why I created Divine Ray, a high-frequency spiritual social app born through three consecutive divine dreams in a single night. I was shown the blueprint—a place where the awakened could find each other, build community, and share light during the most pivotal time in human evolution. Divine Ray is not just an app. It is a consciousness network, a digital temple for the New Earth. And in the months ahead, I'll be pouring energy into expanding it—so star seeds, lightworkers, healers, and visionaries can unite and thrive.

So, what is my future?

It's already happening—etched into every activation, every course, every book, every retreat, every transmission. I'm not here to predict the future, I'm here to co-create it. And I believe what we are building now is far beyond what we can imagine. We are the ones writing the golden scripts of Earth's next chapter.

And it is just beginning.

Dialing the Future – The Greatest Moment in Humanity

It happened in a 1-on-1 session with a client named **Anemona Peres.** Her energy was unlike anything I'd encountered before — and that day, her **High Arcturian aspect came forward.** The frequency in the room intensified. My entire field tuned to hers, and suddenly I was no longer just holding space — **I was being transported.**

Her Arcturian self spoke clearly:

"We are going to show you the coordinates of the greatest moment in human history."

And just like that, I was there — **in a lab,** futuristic but grounded, humming with light intelligence. The air was still, reverent. Standing at the center of this scene was a **scientist — male, focused, brilliant — and seemingly from the Philippines.** But I knew immediately: **he was the one,** the individual whose work would help catalyze the greatest collective awakening.

What I witnessed next was not a vision — it was a blueprint, something real and methodical. **A process to dial the future.**

The Triangle of Time Frequencies

Here's what was shown to me — the method this scientist used to call the future:

1. Anchor Point: The Past

They began by mapping the **star alignment exactly 1000 years ago.**

Each celestial configuration was translated into **a mathematical frequency** — a signature resonance based purely on positioning.

This past frequency became the anchor, the fixed base of the triangle.

2. Midpoint: The Present

Next, they charted the **current star positioning** and again calculated its **precise frequency** based on cosmic placement.

This formed the second point — the midpoint of the triangle — grounding the present in resonance with the past.

3. The Apex: The Future

Then, they chose a point in the future — t**he targeted moment in time** they wished to dial into.

They mapped the **predicted star alignment** for that future era and mathematically **assigned it a frequency.**

This became the apex — the third point of the triangle — the moment they intended to call forward

The Frequency Dialing Algorithm

Once the three frequency points were established — **past, present, future** — I saw them input them into a complex **frequency algorithm.**

This was not a guessing game.

It was **pure frequency triangulation** — each corner of the triangle representing a **dimensional harmonic,** the spatial geometry of time.

The triangle acted like a **frequency prism,** refracting intention through time.

And then... **they dialed.**

They didn't send a message forward — they created a **resonant match**, a vibrational portal — a frequency tunnel — that aligned all three points into a singular vibration. **And the future responded.**

This Is Why You Are Reading This

The Divine has now guided to put this information forward.

"This knowledge must come forward now. It will activate the one who holds the next piece.

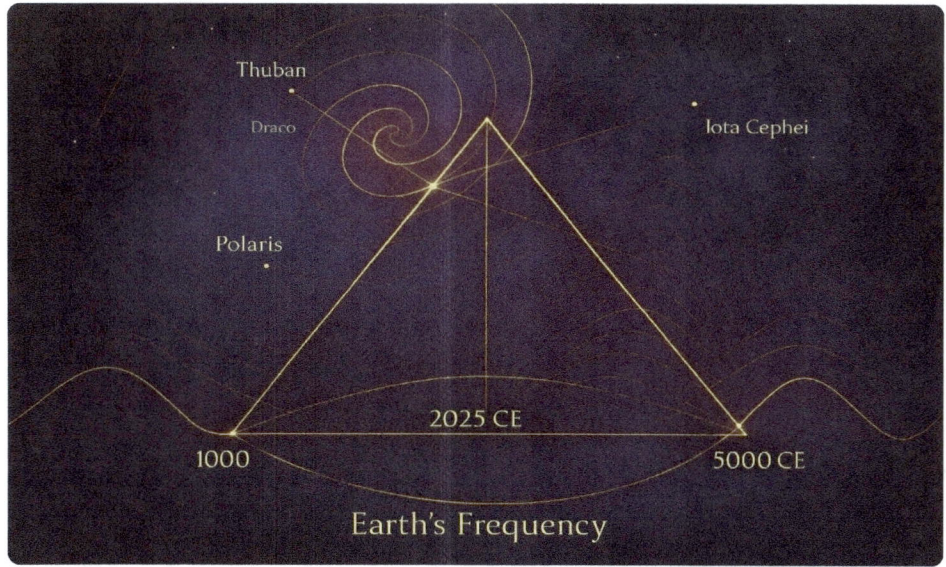

And when the three points unite again — the messenger, the method, and the receiver — the future will open."

I was shown this not to keep it — **but to record it.**

You — yes, you reading this now — may be the scientist.

Or the codekeeper.

Or the harmonic tuner who will complete the circuit.

Or the harmonic tuner who will complete the circuit.

The Divine is guiding the exact people together now — through this book — to fulfill what has been seeded into time.

This isn't fiction.

It's encoded memory.

And now... it has been remembered.

This is how we call the future.

This was a session of a lifetime. And it's no surprise it came through Dr. Anemona Peres—one of the most multidimensional souls I've had the honor of working with. A transpersonal psychologist, clinical hypnotherapist, and urban mystic, Anemona embodies the bridge between science and spirit. After a profound spiritual awakening in her early 40s, she left a two-decade career in international police psychology and academia to follow her soul's calling. Since then, she has become a masterful guide for those seeking to awaken their spiritual gifts and align with their ascension path.

In our session, Anemona brought through her High Arcturian aspect, guiding us on a timeline journey to witness what may become humanity's greatest moment. Her work spans across realms— conscious, subconscious, ancestral, and interdimensional—and she has pioneered her own trauma-informed modality, Hypno-Physis, blending neuroscience, epigenetics, and channeled wisdom from the Pleiadians, Andromedans, Lemurians, and the Sophia Christ lineage.

To learn more about her work, visit www.anemonaperes.com or find her on Facebook, LinkedIn, and the ACCPH directory.

PART VII
THE AWAKENING IS NOW

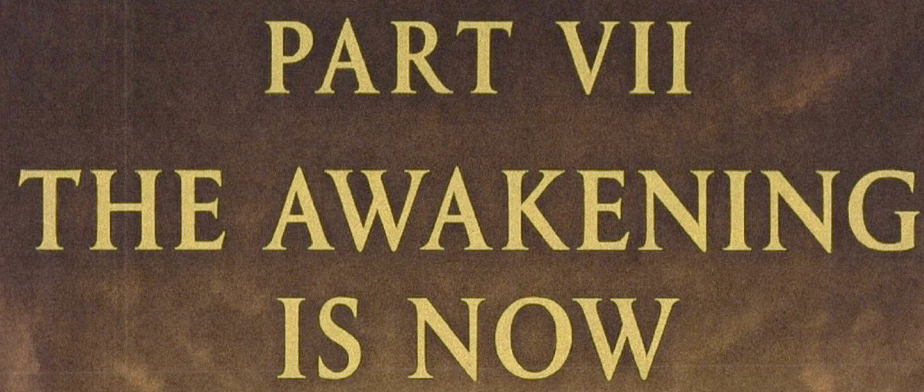

PART VII: THE AWAKENING IS NOW

— You Are the Living Tablet

There comes a moment in every soul's journey where the past, the future, and the present collapse into one thing:

Now.

If you've made it this far through these transmissions, it means something inside you has awakened. Maybe it was subtle. Maybe it roared. Maybe it whispered like a memory you almost forgot. But it stirred — and it was real.

The Tablets were never just ancient.

They were never just mine.

They were yours.

You are the living record.

You are the living scroll.

You are the breath of Source encoded in form,

awakening at the final hour of Earth's great turning.

This moment we are in — right now — is what the Atlanteans saw in prophecy. It is what the Lemurian councils wrote in crystal script. It is what the angelic orders have been preparing for lifetimes.

Ascension is not just a future event.

It's a frequency that already lives inside of you.

And now, it's time to remember.

You Are a Keeper of Light

Everything I have shared — my story, the Tablets, the sessions, the divine visions — was never meant to be a doctrine. It was meant to be a mirror. To remind you that your own soul has a library.

You are a guardian of timelines.

You are a traveler of stars.

You are the golden ink and the scribe.

You are the child of Earth and Heaven — both, not one.

We are not just remembering who we are.

We are reactivating the light-based reality we were always destined to anchor.

And if you're reading these words, your remembering is not accidental. It is divinely timed.

The Earth Awaits Your Embodiment

The Earth has been waiting.

For you to wake.

For you to speak.

For you to love.

The grids are listening.

The crystalline realm is open.

The angels are surrounding you.

And somewhere in the future — or perhaps in the eternal now — your Higher Self is already victorious.

The Mission is Embodiment

You Are Not Alone

As you walk forward now, you are joining the greater convergence of light beings — the soul family, the star seeds, the awakened ones, the ancient architects returning to walk as humans again. Together we are restoring what was once fragmented.

Together we are forming the New Earth Consciousness Grid.

Not as myth. Not as hope. But as truth made manifest.

An Invitation Forward

I invite you to come deeper.

If this book stirred something inside you, then come find me. Our paths have already crossed before — and this reunion is simply another layer of the plan. Join the community, attend a retreat, explore your soul houses, receive your codes, or simply sit in silence and ask:

"Why did I come?"

And listen.

Final Words

The Atlantean prophecy ends with this:

"When the final sun descends and the forgotten ones rise,

a new light will be born on Earth, not from sky nor sea,

but from within the hearts of those who remember."

You are that light.

And the time...

Is Now. — David Starr

ABOUT THE AUTHOR

David Starr is the co-author of the best-selling spiritual guide *Your Higher Power: Accessing Your Divine Gifts*, and author of *Magic Heart Power*, a children's consciousness book and workshop series designed to activate heart-based reality in kids ages 4–14. With a gift for channeling multidimensional teachings, David's work bridges the ancient and the future, helping all ages reconnect to their true soul frequency.

He is the founder of **DavidStarrUnlimited.com,** a global portal offering transformational courses and mentorships that guide spiritual seekers into embodiment, ascension, and divine remembrance. His signature programs — including *The Alchemist Journey, The Evolution Journey, Magic Heart Power,* and *The Ascension Journey* — are beloved for their depth, activation power, and clarity.

David also created **Divine Ray,** a higher consciousness mobile app and spiritual social platform. Download free first QR code android second iPhone.

and hosts **Everything Golden,** a podcast exploring ascension waves, source alignment, channeling, and galactic truth.

In 2025, David hosted a landmark retreat at **Mount Shasta,** where the legendary **Mitchell Hedges Crystal Skull** was present. That retreat sparked a divine remembrance — leading to the channeling and decoding of the *Crystal Tablets of Atlantis*, ancient records encoded in light. These transmissions are now being documented in his upcoming spiritual documentary and the release of this book.

David continues to live in full alignment with his soul mission: to activate the light in others, restore ancient memory, and build the foundations for the New Earth.